Travellers' Dutch

David Ellis is Director of the Somerset Language Centre and co-author of a number of language books

Derktje van der Luit was born in the Netherlands and now lives in London where she teaches Dutch

Dr John Baldwin is Lecturer in Phonetics at University College, London

Other titles in the series

Travellers' Dutch

D. L. Ellis, D. van der Luit

Pronunciation Dr J. Baldwin

Pan Books London and Sydney

Whilst the advice and information in this book is believed to
be true and accurate at the time of going to press, neither the
authors nor the publisher can accept any legal responsibility or
liability for any errors or omissions that may be made

The publishers would like to thank the
Netherlands and Belgian National Tourist Offices for their help
in the preparation of this book

First published 1981 by Pan Books Ltd,
Cavaye Place, London SW10 9PG
2 3 4 5 6 7 8 9
© D. L. Ellis and D. van der Luit 1981
ISBN 0 330 26380 3
Printed and bound in Great Britain by
Hunt Barnard Printing Ltd, Aylesbury, Bucks

Contents

Using the phrase book

- This phrase book is primarily designed to help you get by in the Netherlands, to get what you want or need. However, it could also be used in the Flemish part of Belgium (see map p. 11). It concentrates on the simplest but most effective way you can express these needs in an unfamiliar language.
- The CONTENTS on p. 5 gives you a good idea of which section to consult for the phrase you need.
- The INDEX on p. 155 gives more detailed information about where to look for your phrase.
- When you have found the right page you will be given:
  either – the exact phrase
  or   – help in making up a suitable sentence
  and   – help to get the pronunciation right
- The English sentences in **bold type** will be useful for you in a variety of different situations, so they are worth learning by heart. (See also DO IT YOURSELF, p. 147.)
- Wherever possible you will find help in understanding what Dutch people are saying to *you*, in reply to your questions.
- If you want to practise the basic nuts and bolts of the language further, look at the DO IT YOURSELF section starting on p. 147.
- Note especially these three sections:
  Everyday expressions p. 12
  Shop talk p. 56
  Public notices p. 125
  You are sure to want to refer to them most frequently.
- Once abroad, remember to make good use of the local tourist offices (see p. 26).
  UK addresses:

Netherlands National Tourist Office (NNTO)
Savory and Moore House
2nd Floor
143 New Bond Street
London W1Y 0QS

Belgian National Tourist Office
66 Haymarket
London SW1

A note on the pronunciation system

It is usual in phrase books for there to be a pronunciation section, which tries to teach English-speaking tourists how to pronounce correctly the language of the country they are visiting. Such attempts are based on the argument that correct pronunciation is essential for comprehension. The system in this book, however, is founded on three quite different assumptions: firstly, that it is not possible to describe in print the sounds of a foreign language in such a way that the English speaker with no phonetic training will produce them accurately, or even intelligibly; secondly, that perfect pronunciation is not essential for communication; and lastly that the average visitor abroad is more interested in achieving successful communication than in learning how to pronounce new speech sounds. Observation and experience have shown these assumptions to be justified. The most important characteristic of the present system, therefore, is that it makes no attempt whatsoever to teach the sounds of the other language, but uses instead the nearest English sounds to them. The sentences transcribed for pronunciation are designed to be read as naturally as possible, as if they were ordinary English (of a generally south-eastern variety), and with no attempt to make the words sound 'foreign'. In this way you will still sound quite English but you will at the same time be understood. Practice always helps performance and it is a good idea to rehearse out loud any of the sentences you know you are going to need. When you come to the point of using them, say them with conviction.

In Dutch it is important to stress or emphasize the syllables in italics, just as you would if we were to take as an English example: Little Jack Horner sat in the corner. Here we have ten syllables but only four stresses.

Of course you may enjoy trying to pronounce a foreign language as well as possible and the present system is a good way to start. However, since it uses only the sounds of English, you will very soon need to depart from it as you begin to imitate the sounds you hear the native speaker produce and relate them to the spelling of the other language.

Succes!
souk-cess

John Baldwin, 1980

Everyday expressions

[See also 'Shop talk', p. 56]

• Although you will find the correct greetings listed below, the Dutch commonly use **daag** (duk) to express all of these.

Hello	**Hallo**
	hull*o*
Good morning	**Goede morgen**
	h*oo*-der m*o*r-hen
Good afternoon	**Goede middag**
	h*oo*-der mid-d*u*k
Good day	**Goede dag**
	h*oo*-der duk
Good evening	**Goede avond**
	h*oo*-der *ah*-vent
Good night	**Goede nacht**
	h*oo*-der nukt
Goodbye	**Tot ziens**
	tot *zee*ns
See you later	**Tot straks**
	tot struks
Yes	**Ja**
	yah
Please	**Alstublieft**
	uls-too-bl*eef*t
Great!	**Geweldig!**
	her-wel-dik
Thank you	**Dank u**
	dunk oo
Thank you very much	**Dank u wel**
	dunk oo wel
That's right	**Precies**
	prer-s*ee*s
No	**Nee**
	nay
No, thank you	**Nee, dank u**
	nay' dunk oo
I disagree	**Ik ben het er niet mee eens**
	ik ben et er n*ee*t may ayns
Excuse me	**Pardon**
	par-d*o*n

Don't mention it	**Geen dank**
	hain dunk
That's good	**Dat is goed**
	dut is hoot
That's no good	**Dat is niet goed**
	dut is neet hoot
I know	**Ik weet het**
	ik wait et
I don't know	**Ik weet het niet**
	ik wait et neet
It doesn't matter	**Het geeft niet**
	et hayft neet
Where's the toilet please?	**Waar is het toilet, alstublieft?**
	wahr is et twah-let uls-too-bleeft
How much is that? [point]	**Hoeveel is dat?**
	hoo-vale is dut
Is the service included?	**Is het inclusief bediening?**
	is et in-cloo-seef ber-deening
Do you speak English?	**Spreekt u engels?**
	spraykt oo eng-els
I am sorry . . .	**Het spijt me . . .**
	et spate mer . . .
I don't speak Dutch	**Ik spreek geen nederlands**
	ik sprayk hane nay-der-lunts
I only speak a little Dutch	**Ik spreek maar een beetje nederlands**
	ik sprayk mahr en bayt-yer nay-der-lunts
I don't understand	**Ik begrijp het u niet**
	ik ber-hreyp et oo neet
Please can you . . .	**Kunt u dat alstublieft . . .**
	koont oo dut uls-too-bleeft . . .
repeat that?	**herhalen?**
	her-hah-len
speak more slowly?	**langzamer zeggen?**
	lung-zah-mer zek-en
write it down?	**opschrijven?**
	op-skrey ven
What is this called in Dutch? [point]	**Hoe heet dit in het nederlands?**
	hoo hate dit in et nay-der-lunts

Crossing the border

ESSENTIAL INFORMATION

- Don't waste time just before you leave rehearsing what you are going to say to the border officials – the chances are that you won't have to say anything at all, especially if you travel by air.
  It is more useful to check that you have your documents handy for the journey: passports, tickets, money, travellers' cheques, insurance documents, driving licence and car registration documents.
  Look out for these signs:
DOUANE	(customs)
GRENS	(border)
GRENS POLITIE	(frontier police)

  [For further signs and notices, see p. 125]
- You may be asked routine questions by the customs officials [see below]. If you have to give personal details, see 'Meeting people' p. 16. The other important answer to know is 'Nothing': Niets (neets).

ROUTINE QUESTIONS

Passport?	**Paspoort?**
	p*u*s-port
Insurance?	**Verzekering?**
	ver-*zay*-ker-ing
Registration document?	**Auto papieren?**
(logbook)	*ow*to pah-*pee*-ren
Ticket, please	**Uw kaartje, alstublieft**
	oo *k*art-yeh uls-too-bl*ee*ft
Have you anything to declare?	**Heeft u iets aan te geven?**
	hayft oo eets ahn ter h*a*yven
Where are you going?	**Waar gaat u heen?**
	wahr haht oo hayn
How long are you staying?	**Hoe lang blijft u?**
	hoo lung bleyft oo
Where have you come from?	**Waar komt u vandaan?**
	wahr komt oo vun-d*a*hn

You may have to fill in forms which ask for:

surname	**achternaam**
first name	**voornaam**
maiden name	**meisjesnaam**
place of birth	**geboorteplaats**
date of birth	**geboortedatum**
address	**adres**
nationality	**nationaliteit**
profession	**beroep**
passport number	**paspoort nummer**
issued at	**uitgegeven te**
signature	**handtekening**

Meeting people

[See also 'Everyday expressions', p. 12]

Breaking the ice

Hello	**Hallo**
	hull*o*
Good morning	**Goede morgen**
	h*oo*-der m*o*r-hen
How are you?	**Hoe gaat het?**
	hoo haht et
I am here . . .	**Ik ben hier . . .**
	ik ben h*e*re . . .
on holiday	**met vakantie**
	met vah-*ku*n-tsee
on business	**voor zaken**
	vor z*a*h-ken
Can I offer you . . .	**Mag ik u . . . aanbieden?**
	muk ik oo . . . *ah*n-beeden
a drink?	**iets te drinken**
	eets ter dr*i*nken
a cigarette?	**een sigaret**
	en see-hah-r*e*t
a cigar?	**een sigaar**
	en see-h*a*r
Are you staying long?	**Blijft u lang?**
	bl*ey*ft oo lung

Name

What's your name?	**Hoe heet u?**
	hoo h*a*te oo
My name is . . .	**Ik heet . . .**
	ik h*a*te . . .

Family

Are you married?	**Bent u getrouwd?**
	bent oo het-tr*ou*t

I am . . .	**Ik ben . . .**
	ik ben . . .
married	**getrouwd**
	hert-tr*ou*t
single	**ongetrouwd**
	*o*n-hert-trout
This is . . .	**Dit is . . .**
	dit is . . .
my wife	**mijn vrouw**
	mane vrow
my husband	**mijn man**
	mane mun
my son	**mijn zoon**
	mane zohn
my daughter	**mijn dochter**
	mane d*o*kter
my (boy)friend	**mijn vriend**
	mane vreent
my (girl)friend	**mijn vriendin**
	mane vreen-d*i*n
my colleague (male or female)	**mijn collega**
	mane kol-l*ay*-hah
Do you have any children?	**Heeft u ook kinderen?**
	hayft oo oak k*i*n-der-ren
I have . . .	**Ik heb . . .**
	ik hep . . .
one daughter	**een dochter**
	*ay*n d*o*kter
one son	**een zoon**
	*ay*n zohn
two daughters	**twee dochters**
	tway dokters
three sons	**drie zoons**
	dree zohns
No, I haven't any children	**Nee, ik heb geen kinderen**
	nay ik hep hayn k*i*n-der-ren

Where you live

Are you . . .	Bent u . . .
	bent oo . . .
Dutch?	nederlander/nederlandse?*
	nay-der-lun-ter/nay-der-lunt-ser
Belgian?	belg/belgische?*
	belk/bel-heeser
a Surinamer?	surinamer/surinaamse?*
	soo-ree-nah-mer/soo-ree-nahm-ser
I am . . .	Ik ben . . .
	ik ben . . .
American	amerikaan/amerikaanse*
	ah-may-ree-kahn/ah-may-ree-kahn-ser
English	engelsman/engelse*
[For other nationalities, p. 140]	eng-els-mun/eng-el-ser
I live . . .	Ik woon . . .
	ik woan . . .
in London	in Londen
	in lon-den
in England	in Engeland
	in eng-er-lunt
in the north	in het noorden
	in et norden
in the south	in het zuiden
	in et zo-ee-den
in the west	in het westen
	in et westen
in the east	in het oosten
	in et ohs-ten
in the centre	in het centrum
[For other countries, p. 138]	in et centrem

*Use the first alternative for men, the second for women.

For the businessman and woman

I'm from . . . (firm's name)	**Ik ben van . . .**
	ik ben vun . . .
I have an appointment with . . .	**Ik heb een afspraak met . . .**
	ik hep en *uf*-sprahk met . . .
May I speak to . . .?	**Mag ik met . . . spreken?**
	muk ik met . . . sp*ray*ken
This is my card	**Hier is mijn kaartje**
	here is mane k*a*rt-yer
I'm sorry, I'm late	**Het spijt me dat ik laat ben**
	et spate mer dut ik l*a*ht ben
Can I fix another appointment?	**Kan ik een andere afspraak maken?**
	kun ik en *u*n-der-er *u*f-sprahk m*a*h-ken
I am staying at the hotel . . .	**Ik logeer in hotel . . .**
	ik loh-sh*ee*r in ho-tel . . .

Asking the way

ESSENTIAL INFORMATION

- Keep a look out for all these place names as you will find them on shops, maps and notices.

WHAT TO SAY

Excuse me, please	**Neem me niet kwalijk . . .**
	name mer neet kwah-lek
How do I get . . .	**Hoe kom ik naar . . .**
	hoo kom ik nar . . .
to the airport?	**het vliegveld?**
	et vleek-velt
to Amsterdam?	**Amsterdam?**
	umster-dum
to the beach?	**het strand?**
	et strunt
to the bus station?	**het bus station?**
	et bus stats-see-on
to the Centraal hotel?	**het Centraal Hotel?**
	et cen-trahl hotel
to the Concertgebouw?	**het Concertgebouw?**
	et con-sairt-her-ba-oo
to the Delta Works?	**de Delta Werken?**
	der delta wairken
to the Kalverstraat?	**de Kalverstraat?**
	der kulver-straht
to the market?	**de markt?**
	der markt
to the police station?	**het politiebureau?**
	et poh-lee-tsee-boo-ro
to the post office?	**het postkantoor?**
	et posst-kun-tor
to the railway station?	**het spoorwegstation?**
	et spor-wek-stats-see-on
to the Rijksmuseum?	**het Rijksmuseum?**
	et reyks-moo-sayem

to the Rokin?	**het Rokin?**
	et ro*k*-kin
to the sports stadium?	**het stadion?**
	et sta*h*-dee-on
to the tourist information office?	**het VVV kantoor?**
	et vay-vay-vay kun-t*or*
to Utrecht?	**Utrecht?**
	oo-trekt
Excuse me, please	**Neem me niet kwalijk . . .**
	name mer neet kwa*h*-lek . . .
Is there . . . near by?	**Is hier in de buurt . . .**
	is here in der boort . . .
an art gallery	**een kunst galerij?**
	en k*oo*nst hah-ler-*rey*
a baker's	**een bakker?**
	en b*u*kker
a bank	**een bank?**
	en bunk
a bar	**een bar?**
	en bar
a botanical garden	**een botanische tuin?**
	en bo-ta*h*-nee-ser to-een
a bus stop	**een bushalte?**
	en b*u*s-hulter
a butcher's	**een slager?**
	en sla*h*-her
a café	**een café**
	en cuf-f*a*y
a cake shop	**een banketwinkel?**
	en bunk*et*-winkel
a campsite	**een camping?**
	en camping
a car park	**een parkeerterrein?**
	en par-k*air*-terreyn
a change bureau	**een wissel kantoor?**
	en w*i*ssel kuntor
a chemist's	**een drogist?**
	en dro-h*i*st
a church	**een kerk?**
	en k*air*k
a cinema	**een bioscoop?**
	een bee-os-c*o*pe

Is there . . . near by?	**Is hier in de buurt . . .**
	is here in der boort . . .
a delicatessen	**een delicatessen winkel?**
	en day-lee-kah-tes-sen winkel
a dentist's	**een tandarts?**
	en tunt-arts
a department store	**een warenhuis?**
	en wah-ren-ho-ees
a disco	**een disco**
	en dis-ko
a doctor's surgery	**een dokter?**
	en dok-ter
a dry-cleaner's	**een stomerij?**
	een stomer-rey
a fishmonger's	**een viswinkel?**
	en vis-winkel
a garage (for repairs)	**een garage?**
	en hah-rah-zher
a hairdresser's	**een kapper?**
	en kupper
a greengrocer's	**een groentewinkel?**
	en hroonter-winkel
a grocer's	**een kruidenierswinkel?**
	en kro-ee-der-neers-winkel
a hardware shop	**een ijzerwinkel?**
	en eyzer-winkel
a Health and Social Security Office	**een kantoor Gezondheids en Sociale Zorg Dienst?**
	en kun-tor her-zont-heyts en soh-see-ah-ler zork deenst
a hospital	**een ziekenhuis?**
	en zeeken-ho-ees
a hotel	**een hotel?**
	en ho-tel
an ice-cream parlour	**een ijs-salon?**
	en eys-sah-lon
a laundry	**een wasserij?**
	en wusser-rey
a museum	**een museum?**
	een moo-sayem
a night club	**een nacht club?**
	en nukt cloop

a park	**een park?**
	en park
a petrol station	**een benzinepompstation?**
	en ben-zee-ner-pomp-stats-see-on·
a post box	**een brievenbus?**
	en breeven-bus
a public toilet	**een openbaar toilet?**
	en open-bar twah-let
a restaurant	**een restaurant?**
	en restoran
a (snack) bar	**een snelbuffet?**
	en snel-booffet
a sports ground	**een sportterrein?**
	en sport-terreyn
a supermarket	**een supermarkt?**
	en sooper-markt
a sweet shop	**een snoepwinkel?**
	en snoop-winkel
a swimming pool	**een zwembad?**
	en zwem-but
a telephone (booth)	**een telefoon cel?**
	en telefone cel
a theatre	**een theater?**
	en tay-ah-ter
a tobacconist's	**een sigarenwinkel?**
	en see-hahren winkel
a travel agent's	**een reisbureau?**
	en reys-boo-ro
a youth hostel	**een jeugdherberg?**
	en yerkt-hair-bairk
a zoo	**een dierentuin?**
	en dee-ren-to-een

DIRECTIONS

- Asking where a place is, or if a place is near by, is one thing; making sense of the answer is another.
- Here are some of the most important key directions and replies.

Left	**Links**
	links
Right	**Rechts**
	rekts
Straight on	**Rechtdoor**
	rekt-dor
There	**Daar**
	dar
First left/right	**Eerste links/rechts**
	air-ster links/rekts
Second left/right	**Tweede links/rechts**
	twayder links/rekts
At the crossroads	**Bij de kruisweg**
	bey der kro-ees-wek
At the traffic lights	**Bij de verkeerslichten**
	bey der ver-kairs-lik-ten
At the roundabout	**Bij de rotonde**
	bey der ro-ton-der
At the level crossing	**Bij de overweg**
	bey der over-wek
It's near/far	**Het is dichtbij/ver**
	et is dikt-bey/vair
One kilometre	**Een kilometer**
	ayn kee-lo-mayter
Two kilometres	**Twee kilometer**
	tway kee-lo-mayter
Five minutes . . .	**Vijf minuten . . .**
	veyf mee-nooten . . .
on foot	**lopend**
	lopent
by car	**met de auto**
	met der owto

Take ...	Neem ...
	name ...
the bus	de bus
	der bus
the train	de trein
	der train
the tram	de tram
	der trem

[*For public transport, see p. 116*]

The tourist information office

ESSENTIAL INFORMATION

- Most towns and even some villages in the Netherlands have a tourist information office.
- Look out for the sign shown top right.
- In major towns you will find that in addition the VVV offices also bear the following sign:
- These offices will supply you with information on any region of the Netherlands in the form of leaflets, fold-outs, brochures, lists and plans.
- You may have to pay for some types of document, but this is not usual.
- All offices are open from 9.00 a.m. to 5.00 p.m. weekdays and from 10.00 a.m. to 12.00 p.m. on Saturdays. During the high season, some offices are open during the evenings and on Sunday afternoons.
- For finding a tourist office, see p. 20

WHAT TO SAY

Please, have you got . . .	Heeft u . . . alstublieft?
	.hayft oo . . . uls-too-bleeft
a plan of the town?	**een stadsplan**
	en stats-plun
a list of hotels?	**een hotel lijst**
	en ho-tel leyst
a list of campsites?	**een lijst van camping**
	en leyst vun camping
a list of restaurants?	**een lijst van restaurants**
	en leyst vun res-to-rans
a list of coach excursions?	**een lijst van bus excursies**
	en leyst vun bus ex-cur-sees
a list of events?	**een lijst van evenementen**
	en leyst vun ay-ver-ner-menten
a leaflet on the town?	**een blaadje over de stad**
	en blaht-yer over der stut
a leaflet on the region?	**een blaadje over de omgeving**
	en blaht-yer over der om-hayving

Please, have you got . . .	**Heeft u . . . alstublieft?**
	hayft oo . . . uls-too-bl*ee*ft
a railway timetable?	**een spoorwegboekje**
	en spoor-*wek*-book-yer
a bus timetable?	**een bus dienstregeling**
	en bus d*ee*nst-rayker-ling
In English, please	**In het engels, alstublieft**
	in et *eng*-els uls-too-bl*ee*ft
How much do I owe you?	**Hoeveel ben ik u schuldig?**
	hoo-vale ben ik oo sk*ool*dik
Can you recommend . . .	**Kunt u . . . aanbevelen?**
	koont oo . . . *a*hn-ber-vaylen
a cheap hotel?	**een goedkoop hotel**
	en hoot-k*o*pe ho-t*e*l
a cheap restaurant?	**een goedkoop restaurant**
	en hoot-k*o*pe res-to-r*a*n
Can you make a booking for me?	**Kunt u iets voor me reserveren?**
	koont oo eets vor mer ray-ser-v*ai*ren

LIKELY ANSWERS

You need to understand when the answer is 'No'. You should be able to tell by the assistant's facial expression, tone of voice and gesture; but there are some language clues such as:

No	**Nee**
	nay
I'm sorry	**Het spijt me**
	et spate mer
I don't have a list of hotels	**Ik heb geen lijst van hotels**
	ik hep hayn leyst vun ho-t*e*ls
I haven't got any left	**Ik heb er geen meer**
	ik hep er hayn mair
It's free	**Het is gratis**
	et is hr*a*h-tis

Accommodation

Hotel

ESSENTIAL INFORMATION

- If you want hotel-type accommodation, all the following words in capital letters are worth looking for on name boards:
  HOTEL
  MOTEL
  PENSION (boarding house)
  JEUGDHERBERG (youth hostel)
  ZIMMER (bed and breakfast)
- A list of hotels in the town or district can usually be obtained at the local tourist office [see p. 26].
- All hotels are listed, the cheaper ones having no star rating, while the more luxurious and expensive having proportionally more stars.
- The cost is displayed in the room itself, so you can check it when having a look round before agreeing to stay.
- The displayed cost is for the room itself, per night and not per person. Breakfast is extra and therefore optional.
- Service and VAT (BTW) is always included in the cost of the room, so tipping is voluntary.
- Not all hotels provide meals, apart from breakfast. A breakfast will consist of coffee/tea, bread (usually rolls), cold meats, cheese, jam and fruit.
- An identity document is requested when registering at a hotel and will normally be kept overnight.
- Finding a hotel, see p. 20.

WHAT TO SAY

I have a booking	**Ik heb een gereserveerde kamer** ik hep en her-ray-ser-*vair*-der kah-mer
Have you any vacancies, please?	**Heeft u nog kamers?** hayft oo nok kah-mers
Can I book a room?	**Kan ik een kamer reserveren?** kun ik en kah-mer ray-ser-*vair*en

It's for . . .	Het is voor . . .
	et is vor . . .
one person	één persoon
	ayn pair-sohn
two people	twee personen .
[For numbers, see p. 129]	tway pair-sohnen
It's for . . .	Het is voor . . .
	et is vor . . .
one night	één nacht
	ayn nukt
two nights	twee nachten
	tway nukten
one week	één week
	ayn wake
two weeks	twee weken
	tway waken
I would like . . .	Ik zou graag . . .
	ik zow hrahk . . .
a room	een kamer
	en kah-mer
two rooms	twee kamers
	tway kahmers
with a single bed	met een één-persoonsbed
	met en ayn-pair-sohns-bet
with two single beds	met twee één-persoonsbedden
	met tway ayn-pair-sohns-bed-den
with a double bed	met een tweepersoonsbed
	met en tway-pair-sohns-bet
with a toilet	met toilet
	met twah-let
with a bathroom	met badkamer
	met but-kah-mer
with a shower	met douche
	met doosh
with a cot	met een wieg
	met en week
I'd like . . .	Ik wil het graag met . . . hebben
	ik wil et hrahk met . . . hebben
full board	vol pension
	vol pun-see-on
half board	half (demi) pension
	hulf (day-mee) pun-see-on

Do you serve meals?	**Kunnen we hier eten?**
	koonnen wer here *ay*-ten
At what time is . . .	**Hoe laat is . . .**
	hoo laht is . . .
breakfast?	**het ontbijt?**
	et ont-b*e*yt
lunch?	**de lunch?**
	der lunch
dinner?	**het diner?**
	et -dee-nay
How much is it?	**hoeveel is het?**
	h*o*o-vale is et
Can I look at the room?	**Kan ik de kamer zien?**
	kun ik der k*a*h-mer zeen
I'd prefer a room . . .	**Ik heb liever een kamer . . .**
	ik hep l*ee*ver en k*a*h-mer . . .
at the front/back	**aan de voorkant/achterkant**
	ahn der v*o*r-kunt/ukter-kunt
OK, I'll take it	**Goed, ik neem het**
	hoot ik name et
No thanks, I won't take it	**Nee dank u, deze niet**
	nay dunk oo d*a*zer neet
The key to number (10) please	**De sleutel voor nummer (tien) alstublieft**
	der slertel vor noommer (teen) uls-too-bl*ee*ft
Please, may I have . . .	**Heeft u . . . alstublieft?**
	hayft oo . . . uls-too-bl*ee*ft
a coat hanger?	**een klerenhanger**
	en kl*ai*ren-hung-er
a towel?	**een handdoek**
	en h*u*n-dook
a glass?	**een glas**
	en hlus
some soap?	**een stuk zeep**
	en stook zape
an ashtray?	**een asbak**
	en *u*s-buk
another pillow?	**nog een kussen**
	nok en koossen
another blanket?	**nog een deken**
	nok en d*a*yken

Come in!	**Kom binnen!** kom binnen
One moment, please!	**Een ogenblik alstublieft!** en oh-hen-blik uls-too-bleeft
Please can you . . .	**Kunt u . . . alstublieft?** koont oo . . . uls-too-bleeft
do this laundry/dry-cleaning?	**dit laten wassen/stomen** dit lah-ten wussen/stomen
call me at . . .?	**me om . . . roepen** mer om roopen
help me with my luggage?	**me met mijn bagage helpen** mer met mane bah-hah-sher helpen
call me a taxi for . . .?	**een taxi voor me bestellen** en tuksee vor mer ber-stellen
[For times, see p. 131]	
The bill, please	**De rekening, alstublieft** der rayker-ning uls-too-bleeft
Is service included?	**Is het inclusief bediening?** is et in-cloo-seef ber-dee-ning
I think this is wrong	**Ik denk dat dit verkeerd is** ik denk dut dit ver-kairt is
May I have a receipt?	**Mag ik een kwitantie hebben?** muk ik en kwee-tun-tsee hebben

At breakfast

Some more . . . please	**Nog wat . . . alstublieft** nok wut . . . uls-too-bleeft
coffee	**koffie** koffee
tea	**thee** tay
bread	**brood** broht
butter	**boter** boh-ter
jam	**jam** shem
May I have a boiled egg?	**Mag ik een gekookt ei?** muk ik en her-kohkt ey

LIKELY REACTIONS

Have you an identity document, please?	**Heeft u een identiteitsbewijs, alstublieft?** hayft oo en ee-den-tee-*taits*-ber-weys uls-too-bl*ee*ft
What's your name? [*see p. 16*]	**Wat is uw naam?** wut is oo nahm
Sorry, we're full	**Het spijt me, we zijn vol** et spate mer wer zane vol
I haven't any rooms left	**Ik heb geen kamers meer** ik hep hane k*a*h-mers m*ai*r
Do you want to have a look?	**Wilt u even kijken?** wilt oo *ay*-ven kai-ken
How many people is it for?	**Voor hoeveel personen is het?** vor h*oo*-vale pair-s*oh*-nen is et
From (seven o'clock) onwards	**Vanaf (zeven uur)** vun-*a*f (z*a*y-ven oor)
From (midday) onwards [*For times, see p. 131*]	**Vanaf (twaalf uur's middags)** vun-af (twahlf oor sm*i*d-duks)
It's (30) guilders [*For numbers, see p. 129*]	**Het is (dertig) gulden** et is (d*ai*rtik) hoolden

Camping and youth hostelling

ESSENTIAL INFORMATION
Camping

- Look for the words **CAMPING** or **KAMPEERTERREIN** and this sign.

- Be prepared to have to pay:
  per person
  for the car
  for the tent or caravan plot
  for electricity
  for hot showers
- You must provide proof of identity, such as your passport.
- Officially recognized campsites have a star rating: the more stars, the better equipped.
- Camping is regulated by local and provincial by-laws. Lists are available from the VVV.
- Off-site camping is not permitted.

Youth hostels

- Look for the word: **JEUGDHERBERG**
- You must have a YHA card.
- The charge for the night is the same for all ages, but some hostels are dearer than others.
- You must bring your own sleeping bag lining.
- Accommodation is usually provided in small dormitories.
- Food and cooking facilities vary from place to place and you may also have to help with jobs.
- For buying or replacing camping equipment, see p 54.

WHAT TO SAY

I have a booking	**Ik heb gereserveerd**
	ik hep her-ray-ser-vairt
Have you any vacancies?	**Heeft u nog iets vrij?**
	hayft oo nok eets vrey
It's for . . .	**Het is voor . . .**
	et is vor . . .
one adult/person	**één volwassene/persoon**
	ayn vol-wusserner/pair-sohn
two adults/people	**twee volwassenen/personen**
	tway vol-wussernen/pair-soh-nen
and one child	**en één kind**
	en ayn kint
and two children	**en twee kinderen**
	en tway kin-der-en
It's for . . .	**Het is voor . . .**
	et is vor
one night	**één nacht**
	ayn nukt
two nights	**twee nachten**
	tway nukten
one week	**één week**
	ayn wake
two weeks	**twee weken**
	tway waken
How much is it . . .	**Hoeveel is het . . .**
	hoo-vale is et . . .
for the tent?	**voor de tent?**
	vor der tent
for the caravan?	**voor de caravan?**
	vor der caravan
for the car?	**voor de auto?**
	vor der owto
for the electricity?	**voor de elektriciteit?**
	vor der ay-lek-tree-see-tait
per person?	**per persoon?**
	pair pair-sohn
per day/night?	**per dag/nacht?**
	pair duk/nukt
May I look round?	**Mag ik even rondkijken?**
	muk ik ay-ven rond-kaiken

Do you close the door/gate at night?	**Sluit u de deur/het hek 's avonds?** slo-eet oo der der/et hek sahvents
Do you provide anything ⟶	**Serveert u iets . . .** sair-vairt oo eets . . .
to eat?	**te eten?** ter ay-ten
to drink?	**te drinken?** ter drinken
Do you have . . .	**Heeft u . . .** hayft oo . . .
a bar?	**een bar?** en bar
hot showers?	**warme douches?** warmer dooshes
a kitchen?	**een keuken?** en kerken
a laundry?	**een wasserij?** en wusser-rey
a restaurant?	**een restaurant?** en resto-ran
a shop?	**een winkel?** en winkel
a swimming pool?	**een zwembad?** en zwem-but

[For food shopping, see p. 62, and for eating and drinking out, see p 82]

Where are . . .	**Waar zijn . . .** wahr zane . . .
the dustbins?	**de vuilnisbakken?** der vo-eel-nis-bukken
the showers?	**de douches?** der dooshes
the toilets?	**de toilets?** der twah-lets
At what time must one . . . ⟶	**Hoe laat moet men . . .** hoo laht moot men. . . .
go to bed?	**naar bed?** nar bet
get up?	**opstaan?** op-stahn

Please, have you got . . .   **Heeft u alstublieft**
hayft oo uls-too-bl*ee*ft **. . .**

a broom?   **een bezem?**
en b*a*y-zem

a corkscrew?   **een kurketrekker?**
en k*oo*rker-trekker

a drying-up cloth?   **een theedoek?**
en t*a*y-dook

a fork?   **een vork**
en vork

a fridge?   **een koelkast?**
en k*oo*l-kust

a frying pan?   **een koekepan?**
en k*oo*ker-pun

an iron?   **een strijkijzer?**
en str*ey*k-eyzer

a knife?   **een mes?**
en mess

a plate?   **een bord?**
en bort

a saucepan?   **een pan?**
en pun

a teaspoon?   **een theelepel?**
en t*a*y-laypel

a tin opener?   **een blikopener?**
en bl*i*k-opener

any washing powder?   **wat zeeppoeder?**
wut z*a*pe-pooder

any washing-up liquid?   **een afwasmiddel?**
en *u*fwus-middel

The bill, please   **De rekening, alstublieft**
der r*a*yker-ning uls-too-bl*ee*ft

Problems

The toilet   **Het toilet**
et twah-l*e*t

The shower   **De douche**
der doosh

The tap   **De kraan**
der krahn

The razor point   **Het scheer-contact**
et sk*ai*r-contuct

The light	**Het licht** et likt
... is not working	**... werkt niet** ... wairkt neet
My camping gas has run out	**Ik heb geen kampgas meer** ik hep hane kump-hus mair

LIKELY REACTIONS

Have you an identity document?	**Heeft u een identiteitsbewijs?** hayft oo en ee-den-tee-taits- ber-weys
Your membership card, please	**Uw lidmaatschap-kaart, alstublieft** oo lit-maht-skup-kart uls-too-bleeft
What's your name? [see p. 16]	**Wat is uw naam?** wut is oo nahm
Sorry, we're full	**Het spijt me, we zijn vol** et spate mer wer zane vol
How many people is it for?	**Voor hoeveel personen is het?** vor hoo-vale pair-soh-nen is et
How many nights is it for?	**Voor hoeveel nachten is het?** vor hoo-vale nukten is et
It's (12) guilders ...	**Het is (twaalf) gulden ...** et is (twahlf) hool-den ...
per day/night [For numbers, see p. 129]	**per dag/nacht** pair duk/nukt

Rented accommodation: problem solving

ESSENTIAL INFORMATION

- If you are looking for accommodation to rent, look out for:
  TE HUUR (to let)
  APPARTEMENTEN (flats, rooms)
  KAMERS (rooms)
  VILLA (villa)
  HUIS (house, cottage)
  BUNGALOW (bungalow)
- For arranging details of your let, see 'Hotel' p. 28.
- Key words you will meet if renting on the spot:
  vooruitbetaling (deposit)
  vor-*o*-eet-ber-tahling
  sleutel (key)
  slertèl
- Having arranged your own accommodation and arrived with the key, check the obvious basics that you take for granted.
  Electricity: Voltage? Razors and small appliances brought from home may need adjusting. You may need an adaptor.
  Gas Town gas or bottled gas? Butane gas must be kept indoors, propane gas must be kept outdoors.
  Cooker Don't be surprised to find:
  the grill inside the oven, or no grill at all
  a lid covering the rings which lifts up to form a 'splashback'
  a mixture of two gas rings and two electric rings
  Toilet Mains drainage or septic tank? Don't flush disposable nappies or anything else down the toilet if you are on a septic tank.
  Water Find the stopcock. Check taps and plugs – they may not operate in the way you are used to. Check how to turn on (or light) the hot water.
  Windows Check the method of opening and closing windows and shutters.
  Insects Is an insecticide spray provided? If not, get one locally.
  Equipment See p. 54 for buying or replacing equipment.
  You will probably have an official agent, but be clear in your own mind who to contact in an emergency, even if it is only a neighbour in the first instance.

WHAT TO SAY

My name is . . .	**Mijn naam is . . .** mane nahm is . . .
I'm staying at . . .	**Ik verblijf . . .** ik ver-bleyf . . .
They've cut off . . .	**Ze hebben . . . afgesneden** zer hebben . . . uf-her-snaden
the electricity	**de elektriciteit** der ay-lek-tree-see-tait
the gas	**het gas** et hus
the water	**het water** et wah-ter
Is there . . . in the area?	**Is er een . . . in de omgeving?** is er en . . . in der om-hayving
an electrician	**een elektriciën** en ay-lek-tree-see-en
a plumber	**een loodgieter** en loat-heeter
a gas fitter	**een gasfitter** en hus-fitter
Where is . . .	**Waar is . . .** wahr is . . .
the fuse box?	**de zekering?** der zayker-ring
the stopcock?	**de hoofdkraan?** der hoaft-krahn
the boiler?	**de boiler?** der boiler
the geyser?	**de geiser?** de heyser
Is there . . .	**Is er . . .** is er . . .
bottled gas?	**buta-gas?** boota-hus
a septic tank?	**een beerput?** en bair-poot
central heating?	**centrale verwarming?** cen-trah-ler ver-warming
The cooker	**Het fornuis** et for-no-ees

The hair dryer	**De haardroger**
	der har-dro-her
The heating	**De verwarming**
	der ver-warming
The iron	**Het strijkijzer**
	et streyk-eyzer
The pilot light	**De waakvlam**
	der wahk-vlum
The refrigerator	**De koelkast**
	der kool-kust
The telephone	**De telefoon**
	der telefone
The toilet	**Het toilet**
	et twah-let
The washing machine	**De wasmachine**
	der wus-mashee-ner
... is not working	**... werkt niet**
	... wairkt neet
Where can I get ...	**Waar kan ik ... krijgen?**
	wahr kun ik ... kreyhen
an adaptor for this?	**een hulpstuk voor dit**
	en herlp-sterk vor dit
a bottle of butane gas?	**een fles buta-gas**
	en fles boota-hus
a fuse?	**een zekering**
	en zayker-ring
an insecticide spray?	**een insekten-dodende spuitbus**
	en insekten-doh-den-der spo-eet-bus
a light bulb?	**een gloeilamp**
	en hlooy-lump
The drains	**De afvoer**
	der uf-voor
The sink	**De gootsteen**
	der hoat-stayn
The toilet	**Het toilet**
	et twah-let
... is blocked	**is verstopt**
	... is ver-stopt
The gas is leaking	**Het gas lekt**
	et hus lekt
Can you mend it straightaway?	**Kunt u het direct maken?**
	koont oo et dee-rect mahken

When can you mend it?	**Wanneer kunt u het maken?**
	wun-nair koont oo et mahken
How much do I owe you?	**Hoeveel is het?**
	hoo-vale is et
When is the rubbish collected?	**Wanneer wordt het vuil opgehaald?**
	wun-nair wort et vo-eel
	op-her-hahlt

LIKELY REACTIONS

What's your name?	**Wat is uw naam?**
	wut is oo nahm
What's your address?	**Wat is uw adres?**
	wut is oo ah-dres
There's a shop . . .	**Er is een winkel . . .**
	er is en winkel . . .
in town	**in de stad**
	in der stut
in the village	**in het dorp**
	in et dorp
I can't come . . .	**Ik kan . . . niet komen**
	ik kun . . . neet koh-men
today	**vandaag**
	vun-dahk
this week	**deze week**
	dazer wake
until Monday	**tot maandag**
	tot mahn-duk
I can come . . .	**Ik kan komen . . .**
	ik kun koh-men . . .
on Tuesday	**op dinsdag**
	op dins-duk
when you want	**wanneer u wilt**
	wun-nair oo wilt
Every day	**Elke dag**
	el-ker duk
Every other day	**Om de andere dag**
	om der un-der-er duk
On Wednesdays	**Op woensdag**
	op woons-duk

[*For days of the week, see p. 133*]

General shopping

The chemist's

ESSENTIAL INFORMATION

- Look for the words
  APOTHEEK and **DROGIST**.
  You may also see the following
  signs. A serpent on a staff denotes
  an **apotheek** and a bust of a **gaper**
  (yawner) a **drogist**.
- Medicines (drugs) are available
  only at the **apotheek**.
- Some non-drugs can be bought
  at the **drogist**, at department
  stores or supermarkets.
- Dispensing chemists are
  open Monday to Friday
  8.00 a.m. – 5.30 p.m.
  Chemists take it in turn to
  stay open over the weekend
  and at night.
- Some toiletries can also be
  bought at a **PARFUMERIE** and at hairdressing salons.
- Finding a chemist, see p. 20.

WHAT TO SAY

I'd like . . .	**Ik zou graag . . . hebben** ik zow hrahk . . . hebben
some Alka Seltzer	**wat Alka Seltzer** wut alka seltzer
some antiseptic	**een antiseptisch middel** en *untee*-septees middel
some aspirin	**wat aspirine** wut uspee-*reener*
some bandage	**wat verband** wut ver-*bunt*
some cotton wool	**wat watten** wut *wutten*
some eye drops	**wat oogdruppels** wut *oak*-druppels
some foot powder	**wat voetpoeder** wut *voot*-pooder
some gauze dressing	**wat verbandgaas** wut ver-*bunt*-hahs
some inhalant	**een inhaleermiddel** en in-hah-*lair*-middel
some insect repellent	**een insecten afweermiddel** een insecten *uf*-wair-middel
some lip salve	**wat lippenzalf** wut *lippen*-zulf
some nose drops	**wat neusdruppels** wut *ners*-druppels
some sticking plaster	**wat pleisters** wut *pley*-sters
some throat pastilles	**wat keelpastilles** wut *kale*-pus-til-yes
some vaseline	**wat vaseline** wut vah-ser-*lee*-ner
I'd like something for . . .	**Ik zou graag iets hebben voor . . .** ik zow hrahk eets hebben vor . . .
bites	**beten** b*ay*ten
burns	**brandwonden** br*unt*-wonden
chilblains	**wintervoeten** *winter*-vooten

I'd like something for . . .	**Ik zou graag iets hebben voor . . .**
	ik zow hrahk eets hebben vor . . .
a cold	**verkoudheid**
	ver-kowt-hate
constipation	**constipatie**
	con-stee-pah-tsee
a cough	**hoest**
	hoost
diarrhoea	**diarree**
	dee-ar-ray
ear-ache	**oorpijn**
	or-pain
flu	**griep**
	hreep
sore gums	**zeer tandvlees**
	zair tunt-vlays
sprains	**verstuikingen**
	ver-sto-ee-king-en
stings	**steken**
	stayken
sunburn	**zonnebrand**
	zonner-brunt
travel sickness	**reis ziekte**
	reys zeek-ter
I need . . .	**Ik heb . . . nodig**
	ik hep . . . nodik
some baby food	**wat baby voeding**
	wut baby vooding
some contraceptives	**wat voorbehoedsmiddelen**
	wut vor-ber-hoots-middelen
a deodorant	**een deodorant**
	en day-oh-doh-runt
some disposable nappies	**wat weggooi luiers**
	wut wek-hoy low-ers
some handcream	**wat hand creme**
	wut hunt crem
some lipstick	**een lippenstift**
	en lippen-stift
some make-up remover	**een make-up remover**
	en make-up remover
some paper tissues	**wat papieren tissues**
	wut pah-pee-ren tis-sues

some razor blades	**wat scheermesjes**
	wut sk*ai*r-mes-yes
some safety pins	**wat veiligheidsspelden**
	wut vey-lik-hates-spelden
some sanitary towels	**wat damesverband**
	wut d*a*h-mes-ver-b*u*nt
some shaving cream	**wat scheerzeep**
	wut sk*ai*r-zape
some soap	**wat zeep**
	wut zape
some suntan oil/lotion	**wat zonnebrand olie/creme**
	wut z*o*nner-brunt *o*h-lee/crem
some talcum powder	**wat talkpoeder**
	wut tulk-pooder
some Tampax	**wat Tampax**
	wut t*u*mpux
some (soft) toilet paper	**wat (zacht) toiletpapier**
	wut (zukt) twah-let-pah-peer
some toothpaste	**wat tandpasta**
	wut t*u*nt-pus-tah

[For other essential expressions, see 'Shop talk', p. 56]

Holiday items

ESSENTIAL INFORMATION

- Places to shop at and signs to look for:
  BOEKWINKEL (bookshop, stationery)
  FOTOGRAFIE (films)
  and of course department stores such as:
  DE BIJENKORF
  HEMA
  VROOM EN DREESMANN

WHAT TO SAY

Where can I buy . . .? | **Waar kan ik . . . kopen?**
| wahr kun ik . . . kopen

I'd like . . . | **Ik zou graag . . .**
| ik zow hrahk . . .

a bag | **een tas**
| en tus

a beach ball | **een strandbal**
| en strunt-bul

a bucket | **een emmer**
| en emmer

an English newspaper | **een engelse krant**
| en eng-elser krunt

some envelopes | **wat enveloppen**
| wut enver-loppen

a guide book | **een reisgids**
| en reys-hits

a map (of the area) | **een kaart (van de omgeving)**
| en kart (vun der om-hayving)

some postcards | **wat ansichtkaarten**
| wut unsikt-karten

a spade | **een schop**
| en skop

a straw hat | **een stroohoed**
| en stroh-hoot

a suitcase | **een koffer**
| een koffer

some sunglasses	**een zonnebril**
	en zonner-bril
a sunshade	**een zonnescherm**
	een zonner-skairm
an umbrella	**een paraplu**
	en pah-rah-ploo
some writing paper	**wat schrijfpapier**
	wut skreyf-pah-peer
I'd like . . . [show the camera]	**Ik zou graag . . . hebben**
	ik zow hrahk . . . hebben
a colour film	**een kleurenfilm**
	en kler-ren-film
a black and white film	**een zwart-wit film**
	en zwart-wit film
for prints	**voor afdrukken**
	vor uf-drukken
for slides	**voor dia's**
	vor dee-ahs
12 (24/36) exposures	**twaalf (vierentwintig/zesendertig) opnamen**
	twahlf (veer-en-twintik/zes-en-dairtik) op-nahmen
a standard 8mm film	**een normaal acht millimeter film**
	en normahl ukt mili-mayter film
a super 8 film	**een super acht film**
	en sooper ukt film
some flash bulbs	**een paar flitslampen**
	en par flits-lumpen
This camera is broken	**Deze camera is kapot**
	dazer kahmera is kah-pot
The film is stuck	**De film zit vast**
	der film zit vust
Please can you . . .	**Kunt u dit . . . alstublieft?**
	koont oo dit . . . uls-too-bleeft
develop/print this?	**ontwikkelen/afdrukken**
	ont-wikkelen/uf-drerkken
Please can you load the camera for me?	**Kunt u de film in de camera doen alstublieft?**
	koont oo der film in der kahmera doon uls-too-bleeft

[For other essential expressions, see 'Shop talk' p. 56]

The tobacconist's

ESSENTIAL INFORMATION

- Tobacco is sold where you see these signs: **TABAKSWINKEL** or **SIGARENHANDEL**.
- To ask if there is one near by, see p. 20.
- Most usual brands of tobacco, cigars and cigarettes may be bought at supermarkets and station restaurants.

WHAT TO SAY

A packet of cigarettes . . .	**Een pakje sigaretten . . .** en *puk*-yer see-hah-*re*tten . . .
with filters	**met filter** m*e*t filter
without filters	**zonder filter** zonder filter
king size	**king size** king size
menthol	**menthol** ment*o*l
Those up there . . .	**Die daar boven . . .** dee dar b*o*ven . . .
on the right	**rechts** r*e*kts
on the left	**links** links
These [*point*]	**Deze** d*a*zer
Cigarettes, please	**Sigaretten, alstublieft** see-hah-*re*tten uls-too-bl*ee*ft
100, 200, 300	**honderd, twee honderd, drie honderd** h*o*ndert, tway h*o*ndert, dree h*o*ndert
Two packets	**Twee pakjes** tway p*u*k-yes

Have you got. . .	**Heeft u. . .**
	hayft oo. . .
English cigarettes?	**engelse sigaretten?**
	eng-elser see-hah-retten
American cigarettes?	**amerikaanse sigaretten?**
	ah-may-ree-kahn-ser see-hah-retten
English pipe tobacco?	**engelse pijptabak?**
	eng-elser pape-tah-buk
American pipe tobacco?	**amerikaanse pijptabak?**
	ah-may-ree-kahn-ser pape-tah-buk
rolling tobacco?	**shag?**
	shek
A packet of pipe tobacco	**Een pakje pijptabak**
	en puk-yer pape-tah-buk
That one down there . . .	**Die daar beneden . . .**
	dee dar ber-nayden . . .
on the right	**rechts**
	rekts
on the left	**links**
	links
This one [*point*]	**Deze**
	dazer
A cigar, please	**Een sigaar, alstublieft**
	en see-har uls-too-bleeft
Some cigars, please	**Een paar sigaren, alstublieft**
	en par see-hah-ren uls-too-bleeft
Those [*point*]	**Die**
	dee
A box of matches	**Een doosje lucifers**
	en dohs-yer loo-see-fairs
A packet of pipe cleaners	**Een pakje pijperagers**
[*show lighter*]	en puk-yer paper-rah-hers
A packet of flints	**Een pakje vuursteentjes**
	en puk-yer voor-staynt-yers
Lighter fuel	**Benzine**
	ben-zeener
Lighter gas, please	**Aansteker gas, alstublieft**
	ahn-stay-ker hus uls-too-bleeft

[*For other essential expressions, see 'Shop talk' p. 56*]

Buying clothes

ESSENTIAL INFORMATION

- Look for:
  DAMESKLEDING (women's clothes)
  HERENKLEDING (men's clothes)
  KINDERKLEDING (children's clothes)
  SCHOENENWINKEL (shoe shop)
- Don't buy without being measured first or without trying things on.
- Don't rely on conversion charts of clothing sizes [see p. 145].
- If you are buying for someone else, take their measurements with you.

WHAT TO SAY

I'd like . . .	**Ik zou graag . . . hebben**
	ik zow hrahk . . . hebben
an anorak	**een anorak**
	en *ah*-noh-ruk
a belt	**een riem**
	en reem
a bikini	**een bikini**
	en bikini
a bra	**een BH**
	en bay-hah
a pair of briefs	**een damesbroekje**
	en d*ah*-mes-br*oo*k-yer
a cap (swimming)	**een badmuts**
	en b*u*t-merts
a cap (skiing)	**een skimuts**
	en sk*ee*-merts
a cardigan	**een vest**
	en vest
a coat	**een mantel**
	en m*u*ntel
a dress	**een jurk**
	en yerk
a hat	**een hoed**
	en hoot

a jacket	**een jasje**
	en yus-yer
a pair of jeans	**een spijkerbroek**
	en speyker-brook
a jumper	**een jumper**
	en yum-per
a nightdress	**een nachtjapon**
	en nukt-yah-pon
a pullover	**een pullover**
	een pullover
a pair of pyjamas	**een pyjama**
	en pee-yah-mah
a raincoat	**een regenjas**
	en ray-hen-yus
a shirt	**een overhemd**
	en over-hemt
a pair of shorts	**shorts**
	shorts
a skirt	**een rok**
	en rok
a suit	**een pak**
	en puk
a swimsuit	**een badpak**
	en but-puk
a tee-shirt	**een T-shirt**
	en tee-shirt
a pair of tights	**een mayot**
	en mah-yo
a pair of trousers	**een broek**
	een brook
a pair of underpants	**een onderbroek**
	en onder-brook
I'd like a pair of . . .	**Ik zou graag een paar . . . hebben**
	ik zow hrahk en par . . . hebben
gloves	**handschoenen**
	hunt-skoonen
socks (short/long)	**sokken (kort/lang)**
	sokken (kort/lung)
stockings	**kousen**
	kow-sen

I'd like a pair of . . .	**Ik zou graag een paar . . . hebben**
	ik zow hrahk een par . . . hebben
shoes	**schoenen**
	sk*oo*nen
canvas shoes	**linnen schoenen**
	l*i*nnen sk*oo*nen
sandals	**sandalen**
	sun-d*a*hlen
beach shoes	**strandschoenen**
	str*u*nt-sk*oo*nen
smart shoes	**geklede schoenen**
	her-kl*a*yder sk*oo*nen
boots	**laarzen**
	l*a*rzen
moccasins	**mocassin**
	mok-k*u*s-sin
My size is . . .	**Mijn maat is . . .**
[*For numbers, see p. 129*]	m*a*ne maht is . . .
Can you measure me, please?	**Kunt u me meten, alstublieft?**
	koont oo mer m*a*yten uls-too-bl*ee*ft
Can I try it on?	**Mag ik het aanpassen?**
	muk ik et *a*hn-pussen
It's for a present	**Het is voor een cadeau**
	et is vor en kah-d*o*
These are the	**Dit zijn de maten . . .**
measurements . . .	dit zane der m*a*hten . . .
[*show written*]	
bust/chest	**borst**
	borst
collar	**kraag**
	krahk
hip	**heup**
	herp
leg	**been**
	bayn
waist	**taille**
	tye-yer

Have you got something . . .   Heeft u iets . . .
hayft oo eets . . .

in black?   **in zwart?**
in zwart

in white?   **in wit?**
in wit

in grey?   **in grijs?**
in hreys

in blue?   **in blauw?**
in bla-oo

in brown?   **in bruin?**
in bro-een

in pink?   **in roze?**
in rohs

in green?   **in groen?**
in hroon

in red?   **in rood?**
in rote

in yellow?   **in geel?**
in hale

in this colour? [point] **in deze kleur?**
in dazer kler

in cotton?   **in katoen?**
in kah-toon

in denim?   **in keper?**
in kayper

in leather?   **in leer?**
in lair

in nylon?   **in nylon?**
in ney-lon

in suede   **in suède?**
in soo-ay-der

in wool?   **in wol?**
in wol

in this material? [point] **in dit materiaal?**
in dit mah-teree-ahl

[For other essential expressions, see 'Shop talk', p. 56]

Replacing equipment

ESSENTIAL INFORMATION

- Look for these shops and signs:
  IJZERHANDEL/IJZERWAREN (hardware)
  ELEKTRICITEITSWINKEL (electrical goods)
  HUISHOUDARTIKELEN (household articles)
- In a supermarket look for this display:
  ONDERHOUDSARTIKELEN (household cleaning materials).
- To ask the way to the shop, see p. 20.
- At a campsite try their shop first.

WHAT TO SAY

Have you got . . .	**Heeft u . . .**
	hayft oo . . .
an adaptor?	**een hulpstuk?**
[*show appliance*]	en herlp-sterk
a bottle of butane gas?	**een fles buta-gas?**
	en fles boota-hus
a bottle of propane gas?	**een fles propaan gas?**
	en fles pro-pahn hus
a bottle opener?	**een flesopener?**
	en fles-opener
a corkscrew?	**een kurketrekker?**
	en ker-ker-trekker
any disinfectant?	**een ontsmettingsmiddel?**
	en ont-smettings-middel
any disposable cups?	**wat weggooikoppen?**
	wut wek-hoy-koppen
a drying-up cloth?	**een theedoek?**
	en tay-dook
any forks?	**een paar vorken?**
	en par vorken
a fuse? [*show old one*]	**een zekering?**
	en zayker-ring
an insecticide spray?	**een insektendodend middel?**
	en insekten-dohdent middel
a paper kitchen roll?	**een papieren keukenrol?**
	en pah-pee-ren ker-ken-rol

any knives?	**een paar messen?**
	en par messen
a light bulb? [*show old one*]	**een gloeilampje?**
	een hlooy-lump-yer
a plastic bucket?	**een plastieken emmer?**
	een plus-teeken emmer
a plastic can?	**een plastieken kan?**
	en plus-teeken kun
a scouring pad?	**een pannespons?**
	en punner-spons
a spanner?	**een moersleutel?**
	en moor-slertel
a sponge?	**een spons?**
	en spons
any string?	**wat touw?**
	wut tow
any tent pegs?	**een paar tentpennen?**
	en par tent-pennen
a tin opener?	**een blikopener?**
	en blik-opener
a torch?	**een zaklantaarn?**
	en zuk-lun-tarn
any torch batteries?	**een paar zaklantaarn batterijen?**
	en par zuk-lun-tarn butter-rey-en
a universal plug (for the sink)?	**een algemene stop (voor de gootsteen)?**
	en ulher-mayner stop (vor der hoat-stayn
a washing line?	**een waslijn?**
	en wus-lane
any washing powder?	**wat waspoeder?**
	wut wus-pooder
a washing-up brush?	**een afwasborstel?**
	en ufwus-borstel
any washing-up liquid?	**een vloeibaar afwasmiddel?**
	en vlooy-bar ufwus-middel

[*For other essential expressions, see 'Shop talk', p. 56.*]

Shop talk

ESSENTIAL INFORMATION

- Know your coins and notes
  coins: the guilder is divided into 100 cents. Some of these coins have 'popular' names: 5 cents **een stuiver**, 10 cents **een dubbeltje**, 25 cents **een kwartje**, Fl. 2.50 **een rijksdaalder**
  notes Fl. 5, Fl. 10, Fl. 25, Fl. 1000
- Know how to say the important weights and measures. You will hear grams, ounces, kilos and pounds used in shops and markets. The metric Dutch pound **pond** (pont) is ten per cent more than the UK pound and there are exactly 2 **pond** in 1 kilo. The metric Dutch ounce **ons** (ons) is equivalent to 100 grams. Throughout the book you will find that we have used the colloquial Dutch expressions (i.e. ½ oz, 1 oz, 1 lb) to translate grams and kilograms, as they are both more widely used and simpler to say.

  [*For numbers, see p. 129*]

50 grams/½ oz	**vijftig gram/een half ons**
	veyftik hrum/en hulf ons
100 grams/1 oz	**honderd gram/één ons**
	hondert hrum/ayn ons
200 grams/2 oz	**tweehonderd gram/twee ons**
	tway-hondert hrum/tway ons
250 grams/½ lb	**tweehonderdvijftig gram/een half pond**
	tway-hondert-veyftik hrum/en hulf pont
½ kilo/1 lb	**een halve kilo/één pond**
	en hulver kilo/ayn pont
1 kilo/2 lbs	**één kilo/twee pond**
	ayn kilo/tway pont
2 kilos	**twee kilo**
	tway kilo
½ litre	**een halve liter**
	een hulver leeter
1 litre	**één liter**
	ayn leeter
2 litres	**twee liter**
	tway leeter

- In small shops don't be surprised if customers, as well as the shop assistant say 'hello' and 'goodbye' to you.

CUSTOMER

Hello	**Hallo**
	hullo
Good morning	**Goede morgen**
	hoo-der mor-hen
Good afternoon	**Goede middag**
	hoo-der mid-duk
Goodbye	**Tot ziens**
	tot zeens
I'm just looking	**Ik kijk even**
	ik keyk ay-ven
Excuse me	**Excuseer me**
	ex-coo-sair mer
How much is this/that?	**Hoeveel is dit/dat?**
	hoo-vale is dit/dut

What's that?	**Wat is dat?**
	wut is dut
What are those?	**Wat zijn dat?**
	wut zane dut
Is there a discount?	**Is er korting op?**
	is er korting op
I'd like that, please	**Ik wil dat graag hebben, alstublieft**
	ik wil dut hrahk hebben uls-too-bleeft
Not that	**Dat niet**
	dut neet
Like that	**Zoals dat**
	zo-uls dut
That's enough, thank you	**Dat is genoeg, dank u**
	dut is her-nook dunk oo
More please	**Wat meer alstublieft**
	wut mair uls-too-bleeft
Less please	**Wat minder alstublieft**
	wut min-der uls-too-bleeft
That's fine	**Dat is fijn**
	dut is fane
OK	**OK**
	okay
I won't take it, thank you	**Ik neem het niet, dank u**
	ik name et neet dunk oo
It's not right	**Het is niet goed**
	et is neet hoot
Thank you very much	**Dank u wel**
	dunk oo wel
Have you got something . . .	**Heeft u iets . . .**
	heyft oo eets . . .
better?	**beters?**
	bayters
cheaper?	**goedkopers?**
	hoot-kopers
different?	**anders?**
	unders
larger?	**groters?**
	hroh-ters
smaller?	**kleiners?**
	kleyners

At what time do you . . .	**Hoe laat gaat u . . .**
	hoo laht haht oo . . .
open?	**open?**
	*o*pen
close?	**dicht?**
	dikt
Can I have a bag, please?	**Mag ik een zak, alstublieft?**
	muk ik en z*u*k uls-too-bl*ee*ft
Can I have a receipt?	**Mag ik een kwitantie?**
	muk ik en kwee-t*u*n-tsee
Do you take . . .	**Neemt u . . . aan?**
	naymt oo . . . ahŋ
English/American money?	**engels/amerikaans geld**
	*e*ng-els/ah-may-ree-k*a*hns helt
travellers' cheques?	**reischeques**
	r*e*ys-cheques
credit cards?	**credietkaarten**
	cred*ee*t-karten
I'd like . . .	**Ik zou graag . . .**
	ik zow hrahk . . .
one like that	**één zoals dat**
	ayn zo-uls dut
two like that	**twee zoals dat**
	tway zo-uls dut

SHOP ASSISTANT

Can I help you?	**Kan ik u helpen?**
	kun ik oo helpen
What would you like?	**Wat wilt u hebben?**
	wut wilt oo hebben
Will that be all?	**Is dat alles?**
	is dut ul-les
Anything else?	**Iets anders?**
	eets unders
Would you like it wrapped?	**Wilt u het ingepakt hebben?**
	wilt oo et in-her-pukt hebben
Sorry, none left	**Tot mijn spijt, uitverkocht**
	tot mane spate o-eet-ver-kokt
I haven't got any	**Ik heb geen**
	ik heb hane
I haven't got any more	**Ik heb geen meer**
	ik hep hane mair
How many do you want?⎤	**Hoeveel wenst u?**
How much do you want?⎦	hoo-vale wenst oo
Is this enough?	**Is dit genoeg?**
	is dit her-nook

Shopping for food

Bread

ESSENTIAL INFORMATION

- Finding a baker's, see p. 18.
- Key words to look for:
  BAKKERIJ (baker's)
  BAKKER (baker)
  BROOD (bread)
- Supermarkets of any size and general stores nearly always sell bread.
- Opening times are usually 8.30 a.m. – 5.30 p.m.; early closing time varies slightly locally.
- The most characteristic type of loaf is the 'French stick', which comes in two sizes: large and small.
- Most bread is sold unsliced in both bakeries and supermarkets. However, if you prefer your bread sliced **gesneden** (her-sn*a*yden), hand the loaf to the assistant and she will slice it for you. You will have to pay a small charge for this service.

WHAT TO SAY

A loaf (like that)	**Een brood (zoals dat)**
	en brote (zo-uls dut)
A whole loaf	**Een heel brood**
	en hale brote
A half loaf	**Een half brood**
	en hulf brote
A white loaf	**Een wit brood**
	en wit brote
A wholemeal loaf	**Een tarwe brood**
	en tar-wer brote
A currant loaf	**Een krentenbrood**
	en krenter-brote
A packet of pumpernickel	**Een pakje roggebrood**
	en puk-yer rok-her-brote
A bread roll	**Een broodje**
	een brote-yer
A currant bun	**Een krentenbol**
	en krenter-bol
Two loaves	**Twee broden**
	tway broden
Three rolls	**Drie broodjes**
	dree brote-yers
Four currant buns	**Vier krentenbollen**
	veer krenter-bollen
Two packets of rusks	**Twee rollen beschuit**
	tway rollen ber-sko-eet
A French stick	**Een stokbrood**
	en stok-brote

[*For other essential expressions, see 'Shop talk' p. 56*]

Cakes

ESSENTIAL INFORMATION

- Key words to look for:
  BANKETBAKKERIJ (cake shop)
  BANKETBAKKER (cake/pastry maker)
  GEBAK (pastries/cakes)
- To find a cake shop, see p. 20.
- THEE-SALON: a place to buy cakes and have a drink, usually in the afternoon. See also p. 82 'Ordering a drink'.

WHAT TO SAY

The type of cakes you find in the shops may vary from region to region but the following are the most common; cake is *not* bought per slice, but gâteau is.

een cake en cake	a plain butter cake; size about 300 – 700 grams
een rozijnen cake en roh-*zey*nen cake	a raisin cake
een citroen cake en cit*roo*n cake	a lemon cake
een appeltaart en *u*ppel-tart	an apple tart
een slagroomtaart en sl*u*k-rome-tart	a cream tart/gâteau
een vruchtentaart en vr*u*kten-tart	a fruit tart/gâteau
een kwarktaart en kwark-tart	a cheese (cream) cake/gâteau
roomsoezen *ro*me-soozen	éclairs
slagroomgebakjes sl*u*k-rome-her-b*u*k-yers	cream pastries
vruchtengebakjes vr*u*kten-her-buk-yers	fruit pastries
amandelbroodjes um-m*u*ndel-brote-yers	almond rolls

Medium-size cakes and pastries are usually bought by number:

One almond roll, please	**Eén amandelbroodje, alstublieft** ayn um-m*u*ndel-brote-yer uls-too-bl*ee*ft
Two almond rolls, please	**Twee amandelbroodjes, alstublieft** tway um-m*u*ndel-brote-yers uls-too-bl*ee*ft

Biscuits are bought by weight:

200 grams of biscuits	**Twee ons koekjes** tway ons k*oo*k-yers
250 grams mixed biscuits	**Een half pond gemengde koekjes** en hulf pont her-meng-der k*oo*k- yers

[*For further details on Dutch weights, see 'Shop talk', p. 56*]

You may want to buy a larger cake by the slice:

One slice of apple cake	**Eén punt appelgebak** ayn p*e*rnt *u*ppel-her-buk
Two slices of cheesecake	**Twee punten kwarktaart** tway p*e*rn-ten kw*a*rk-tart

You may also say:

A selection, please	**Wat gebak, alstublieft** wut her-b*u*k uls-too-bl*ee*ft

[*For other essential expressions, see 'Shop talk', p. 56*]

Ice-cream and sweets

ESSENTIAL INFORMATION

- Key words to look for:
  IJS (ice-cream)
  IJS-SALON (ice-cream parlour)
  BONBONS en CHOCOLADE (chocolates)
  BANKETBAKKERIJ (pastry maker's)
  BANKETBAKKER (pastry maker)
  SUIKERWERKEN (sweet shop)
- Best known ice-cream brand-names are:
  OLA
  CAMPINA
  CARACA
  VENEZIA
- When buying ice-cream, specify what price cone or tub you want.
- Pre-packed sweets are available in general stores and supermarkets.

WHAT TO SAY

A . . . ice, please	**Een . . . ijsje, alstublieft**
	en . . . eys-yer uls-too-bleeft
banana	**bananen**
	bah-nah-nen
chocolate	**chocolade**
	shocolah-der
mocha	**mokka**
	mokka
pistachio	**pistache**
	peestush
strawberry	**aardbeien**
	ard-bey-yen
vanilla	**vanille**
	vun-il-yer
One (50 cent) cone	**Eén van (vijftig)**
	ayn vun (veyftik)
Two (Fl. 1) cones	**Twee van (één gulden)**
	tway vun (ayn hoolden)

Two (Fl. 1.50) tubs	**Twee bekertjes van (één vijftig)**
	tway bakert-yes vun (ayn vetftik)
A lollipop	**Een lollie**
	en lollee
A packet of ...	**Een pakje ...**
	en puk-yer ...
100 grams of ...	**Eén ons ...**
	ayn ons ...
200 grams of ...	**Twee ons ...**
	tway ons ...

[*For further details of Dutch weights, see 'Shop talk', p. 56*]

chewing gum	**kauw gom**
	cow hom
chocolates	**bonbons**
	bonbons
liquorice	**dropjes**
	drop-yers
mints	**pepermunt**
	paper-munt
sweets	**snoepjes**
	snoop-yers
toffees	**toffees**
	toffays

[*For other essential expressions, see 'Shop talk' p. 56*]

In the supermarket

ESSENTIAL INFORMATION

- The place to ask for: [*see p. 20*]
  EEN SUPERMARKT (supermarket)
  EEN KRUIDENIERSWINKEL (grocery shop)
- Key instructions on signs in the shop:
  INGANG (entrance)   **KASSA** (cash desk)
  UITGANG (exit)   **RECLAME** (on offer)
  GEEN INGANG (no entry)   **ZELFBEDIENING** (self-service)
  GEEN UITGANG (no exit)
- Opening times vary but in general are weekdays between 8.30/
  9.00 a.m. – 5.30/6.00 p.m., and Saturdays 8.30/9.00 a.m. – 4.00
  p.m. Some shops have introduced late closing and you will find
  that others are closed during lunchtime.
- No need to say anything in a supermarket, but ask if you can't
  see what you want.
- For non-food items see 'Replacing equipment', p. 54.

WHAT TO SAY

Excuse me, please	**Pardon**
	pardon
Where is . . .	**Waar is . . .**
	wahr is . . .
the bread?	**het brood?**
	et brote
the butter?	**de boter?**
	der boter
the cheese?	**de kaas?**
	der kahs
the chocolate?	**de chocolade?**
	der shocol*a*h-der
the coffee?	**de koffie?**
	der *coffee*
the cooking oil?	**de kookolie?**
	der *coke*-oh-lee
the fish?	**de vis?**
	der vis
the frozen food?	**het diepvries voedsel?**
	et d*ee*p-frees *voo*tsel
the fruit?	**het fruit?**
	et fro-eet

the jam?	**de jam?**
	der shem
the meat?	**het vlees?**
	et vlays
the milk?	**de melk?**
	der melk
the mineral water?	**het mineraal water?**
	et mee-ner-rahl wah-ter
the salt?	**het zout?**
	et zowt
the sugar?	**de suiker?**
	der so-ee-ker
the tea?	**de thee?**
	der tay
the vinegar?	**de azijn?**
	der ah-zeyn
the wine?	**de wijn?**
	der weyn
the yogurt?	**de yoghurt?**
	der yo-hurt
Where are . . .	**Waar zijn . . .**
	wahr zane . . .
the biscuits?	**de koekjes?**
	der kook-yers
the crisps?	**de chips?**
	der chips
the eggs?	**de eieren?**
	der ey-er-en
the fruit juices?	**de vruchtensappen?**
	der vrukten-suppen
the pastas?	**de meelsoorten?**
	der mail-sorten
the soft drinks?	**de frisdranken?**
	der fris-drunken
the sweets?	**de snoepjes?**
	der snoop-yers
Where are . . .	**Waar is . . .**
	wahr is . . .
the tinned vegetables?	**de blikgroente?**
	der blik-hroonter
the vegetables?	**de groente?**
	der hroonter

[*For other essential expressions, see 'Shop talk' p. 56*]

Picnic food

ESSENTIAL INFORMATION

● Key words to look for:
DELICATESSEN ⎤ delicatessen
VLEESWAREN ⎦
Weight guide: 150 grams of prepared salad per two people, if eaten as a starter to a substantial meal; 100 grams of prepared salad per person, if to be eaten as the main part of a picnic-type meal.

WHAT TO SAY

A slice of . . .	**Een plak . . .**
	en pluk . . .
Two slices of . . .	**Twee plakken . . .**
	tway plukken . . .
roast beef	**rosbief**
	ros-beef
roast pork	**varkens rollade**
	var-kens rollah-der
tongue	**tong**
	tong
ham	**ham**
	hum
liver sausage	**leverworst**
	layver-worst
garlic sausage	**knoflook worst**
	knof-loke worst
salami	**salami**
	sah-lah-mee
100 grams of . . .	**Eén ons . . .**
	ayn ons . . .
150 grams of . . .	**Anderhalf ons . . .**
	under-hulf ons . . .
200 grams of . . .	**Twee ons . . .**
	tway ons . . .
300 grams of . . .	**Drie ons . . .**
	dree ons . . .

[*For further details of Dutch weights, see 'Shop talk' p. 56*]

potato salad	**aardappelsla**
	ar-duppel-slah
herring salad	**haring sla**
	hah-ring slah
Russian salad	**huzaren sla**
	hoo-zah-ren slah
coleslaw	**koolsla**
	kohl-slah
olives	**olijven**
	oh-ley-ven ·

You might also like to try some of these:

een stuk rookworst
en sterk roke-worst
a piece of smoked sausage (best eaten hot)

een zoute nieuwe haring
en zowter nee-wer hahring
a salted fresh herring

en gerookte paling
en her-roke-ter pah-ling
a smoked eel

een Frankfurter
en frunk-foorter
a Frankfurter sausage

een stuk boterhammenworst
en sterk boter-hummer-worst
some luncheon meat

wat rookvlees
wut roke-vlays
some smoked beef (thin, salty slices)

wat gerookt makreel
wut her-roke-ter mah-krayl
some smoked mackerel

wat zult
wut zult
some brawn: pork (boar's flesh) pickled in vinegar

wat vis-sla
wut vis-slah
some fish salad

wat champignon-sla
wut shum-peen-yon-slah
some mushroom salad

wat gehakt
wut her-hukt
cold, spicy minced meat (pork or beef)

wat worstsla
wut worst-slah
some sausage salad

wat kippesla
wut kipper-slah
some chicken salad

wat kaassla
wut kahs-slah
some cheese salad

Goudse kaas (belegen)
howtser kahs (berlay-hen)
Gouda cheese (mature)

Edammer kaas	Edam cheese
ay-*du*mmer kahs	
Leidse kaas	Leiden cheese (cumin seed cheese)
*ley*t-ser kahs	
nagelkaas	clove cheese
nah-hel kahs	
Limburgse kaas	Limburger (piquant) cheese
*lim*burg-ser kahs	

Fruit and vegetables

ESSENTIAL INFORMATION

- Key words to look for:
  FRUIT (fruit)
  FRUITHANDELAAR (fruiterer)
  GROENTEN (vegetables)
- If possible, buy fruit and vegetables in the market, where they are cheaper and fresher than in the shops. Open-air markets are held once a week in most areas, usually in the mornings.
- It is customary for you to choose your own fruit and vegetables at the market and for the stallholder to weigh and price them. You must take your own shopping bag as paper and plastic bags are not normally provided.
- Weight guide: 1 kilo of potatoes is sufficient for six people for one meal.

  [*For further details of Dutch weights, see 'Shop talk', p. 56*]

WHAT TO SAY

1/2 kilo of . . .	**Eén pond . . .**
	ayn pont . . .
1 kilo of . . .	**Eén kilo . . .**
	ayn *ki*lo . . .
2 kilos of . . .	**Twee kilo . . .**
	tway *ki*lo . . .
apples	**appels**
	*u*ppels

apricots	**abrikozen**
	ah-bree-k*o*zen
bananas	**bananen**
	bah-n*ah*-nen
bilberries	**bosbessen**
	b*o*s-bessen
cherries	**kersen**
	k*ai*rsen
grapes (white/black)	**druiven (witte/zwarte)**
	dr*o*-ee-ven (w*i*tter/zw*a*rter)
greengages	**reineclaude**
	rayner-cl*ow*der
mulberries	**moerbeien**
	m*oo*r-bey-en
oranges	**sinaasappels**
	s*ee*-nahs-uppels
pears	**peren**
	p*ay*ren
peaches	**perziken**
	p*ai*rzi-ken
plums	**pruimen**
	pr*o*-ee-men
raspberries	**frambozen**
	frum-b*o*zen
strawberries	**aardbeien**
	*a*rd-bey-yen
A pineapple, please	**Een ananas, alstublieft**
	en *u*n-ah-nus uls-too-bl*ee*ft
A grapefruit	**Een grapefruit**
	en grape-fruit
A melon	**Een meloen**
	en mer-l*oo*n
A water melon	**Een watermeloen**
	en w*a*h-ter-mer-loon
250 grams of . . .	**Een half pond . . .**
	en hulf pont . . .
1/2 kilo of . . .	**Eén pond . . .**
	ayn pont . . .
1 kilo of . . .	**Eén kilo . . .**
	ayn k*i*lo . . .

1½ kilos of . . .   **Anderhalve kilo . . .**
                                  under-hulver *ki*lo . . .

[*For further details of Dutch weights, see 'Shop talk' p. 56*]

aubergines	**aubergines**
	oh-ber-sheens
broad beans	**tuinbonen**
	t*o*-een-bonen
carrots	**wortels**
	wor-tels
green beans	**slabonen**
	sl*ah*-bonen
leeks	**prei**
	prey
mushrooms	**champignons**
	shum-peen-y*o*ns
onions	**uien**
	*o*we-yen
peas	**doperwten**
	dop*air*-ten
podded peas	**peultjes**
	p*e*rlt-yers
potatoes	**aardappels**
	*a*r-duppels
red cabbage	**rode kool**
	roder kohl
shallots	**sjalotten**
	shah-l*o*t-ten
spinach	**spinazie**
	spee-n*ah*-zee
tomatoes	**tomaten**
	toh-m*ah*-ten
A bunch of . . .	**Een bosje . . .**
	en b*o*s-yer . . .
parsley	**peterselie**
	pa-ter-s*ay*lee
radishes	**radijs**
	rah-d*e*ys
A garlic	**Een knoflook**
	en kn*o*f-loke
A lettuce	**Een krop sla**
	en krop slah
A stick of celery	**Een bleekselderij**
	en blake-selder-ray

A cauliflower	**Een bloemkool**
	en bl*oo*m-koh*l*
A cabbage	**Een kool**
	en kohl
A cucumber	**Een komkommer**
	en kom-kommer
A turnip	**Een witte raap**
	en w*i*tter rahp
Like that, please	**Zoals dat, alstublieft**
	zo-uls dut uls-too-bl*ee*ft

Vegetables and fruit which may not be familiar:

andijvie	endive, a salad plant with a bitter
un-d*ey*-vee	flavour
Brussels lof	chicory, used in winter salads,
br*u*ssels lof	same family as the above
knolselderij	celeriac, a variety of celery
kn*o*l-selder-rey	
postelein	purslane, a salad herb
pos-ter-leyn	

[For other essential expressions, see 'Shop talk' p. 56]

Meat

ESSENTIAL INFORMATION

- Key words to look for:
  SLAGERIJ (butcher's)
  SLAGER (butcher)
- Weight guide: 125–200 grams of meat per person for one meal.
  The diagrams below are to help you make sense of labels on
  counters, windows and supermarket displays, and decide which
  cut or joint to have. Translations don't help, and you don't need
  to say the Dutch word involved.
- Lamb and mutton are expensive in Holland.

WHAT TO SAY

For a joint, choose the type of meat and then say how many people
it is for:

Some beef, please	**Wat rundvlees, alstublieft**
	wut r*u*nt-vlays uls-too-bl*ee*ft
Some lamb	**Wat lamsvlees**
	wut l*u*ms-vlays
Some mutton	**Wat schapevlees**
	wut sk*a*h-per-vlays
Some pork	**Wat varkensvlees**
	wut v*a*rkens-vlays
Some veal	**Wat kalfsvlees**
	wut k*u*lfs-vlays
A joint . . .	**Groot stuk vlees . . .**
	hrote sterk vlays . . .
for two people	**voor twee personen**
	vor tway pair-s*o*hnen
for four people	**voor vier personen**
	vor veer pair-s*o*hnen
for six people	**voor zes personen**
	vor zes pair-s*o*hnen

For steak, liver and kidneys do as above:

Some steak, please	**Wat biefstuk, alstublieft**
	wut b*ee*f-sterk uls-too-bl*ee*ft

Beef Rund

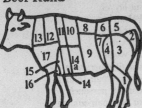

1 Achterschenkel	10 Fijne rib
2 Muis	11 Dikke rib
3 Platte bil	12 Onderrib
4 Spierstuk	13 Hals
5 Staartstuk	14 Naborst
6 Dikke lende	14a Dunne borst
7 Liesstuk (ezeltje)	15 Borst
8 Dunne lende	16 Puntborst
9 Vang	17 Schouder met voorschenkel

Veal Kalf

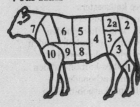

1 Achterschenkel
2 Platte fricandeau met staartstuk
2a Dikke lende
3 Kalkoenstuk met liesstuk
4 Lende met vang (nierstuk en koteletten)
5 Ribstuk (fijne rib) (koteletten)
6 Ribstuk (dikke rib)
7 Onderrib met hals
8 Dunne borst
9 Borst
10 Schouder met voorschenkel

Pork Varken

1 Ham (vleeskant)
2 Rugspek
3 Buik (mager spek met broek)
4 Schouder
5 Kop met kinnebak

Lamb Lam

1 Bout met been
2 Lamszadel
3 Lamsrug
4 Lamsborst
5 Schouder
6 Nek

Some liver	**Wat lever**
	wut l*a*yver
Some kidneys	**Wat nieren**
	wut n*ee*-ren
Some sausages	**Wat worst**
	wut worst
for three people	**voor drie personen**
	vor dree pair-s*o*hnen
for five people	**voor vijf personen**
	vor veyf pair-s*o*hnen

For chops do it this way:

Two veal escalopes	**Twee kalfsoesters**
	tway k*u*lfs-oosters
Three pork chops	**Drie varkenskarbonaden**
	dree v*a*rkens-karboh-nahden
Four mutton chops	**Vier schaapskarbonaden**
	veer sk*a*hps-karboh-nahden
Five lamb chops	**Vijf lamskarbonaden**
	veyf l*u*ms-karboh-nahden

You may also want:

A chicken	**Een kip**
	en kip
A rabbit	**Een konijn**
	en koh-n*e*yn
A tongue	**Een tong**
	en tong

Other essential expressions [*see also p. 56*]

Please can you . . .	**Kunt u het . . . alstublieft?**
	koont oo et . . . uls-too-bl*ee*ft
mince it?	**malen**
	m*a*hlen
dice it?	**tot dobbelstenen snijden**
	tot d*o*bbel-staynen sn*a*den
trim the fat?	**vet afsnijden**
	vet *u*f-sn*a*den

Fish

ESSENTIAL INFORMATION

- The place to ask for: **EEN VISWINKEL** (a fishmonger's)
- Markets and large supermarkets usually have fresh fish stalls. Weight guide 250 grams minimum per person, for one meal, of fish bought on the bone.

  i.e. 1/2 kilo/500 grams for 2 people
  1 kilo for 4 people
  1½ kilos for 6 people

WHAT TO SAY

Purchase large fish and small shellfish by weight:

½ kilo of . . .	**Eén pond . . .** ayn pont . . .
1 kilo of . . .	**Eén kilo . . .** ayn kilo . . .
1½ kilos of . . .	**Anderhalve kilo . . .** under-hulver kilo . . .
cod	**kabeljauw** kahbel-yow
eel	**paling** pahling
haddock	**schelvis** skelvis
herring	**haring** hah-ring
pike	**snoek** snook
plaice	**schol** skol
turbot	**tarbot** tarbot
mussels	**mosselen** mossel-en
prawns	**garnalen** har-nahlen
shrimps	**kleine garnalen** kleyner har-nahlen

Some large fish can be purchased by the slice:

One slice of . . .	Eén moot . . .
	ayn mote . . .
Two slices of . . .	Twee moten . . .
	tway moten . . .
Six slices of . . .	Zes moten . . .
	zes moten . . .
salmon	zalm
	zulm
cod	kabeljauw
	kahbel-yow
haddock	schelvis
	skelvis
tuna	tonijn
	toh-neyn

For some shellfish and 'frying pan' fish specify
the number you want:

A crab, please	Een krab, alstublieft
	en krup uls-too-bleeft
A lobster	Een zeekreeft
	en zay-kraft
A scallop	Een kammossel
	en kum-mossel
A plaice	Een schol
	en skol
A whiting	Een wijting
	en waiting
A trout	Een forel
	en foh-rel
A sole	Een tong
	en tong
A mackerel	Een makreel
	en mah-krayl
A herring	Een haring
	en hahring

Other essential expressions [*see also p. 56*]

Please can you . . .	Kunt u . . . alstublieft
	koont oo . . . uls-too-bl*ee*ft
take the heads off?	de k*o*ppen afsnijden?
	de k*o*ppen *u*f-sn*a*den
clean them?	ze schoonmaken?
	zer sk*o*ne-mahken
fillet them?	ze fileren?
	zer fee-l*ai*ren

Eating and drinking out

Ordering a drink

ESSENTIAL INFORMATION

- The place to ask for [see p. 20]
  EEN CAFÉ
- By law, the price list of drinks (**TARIEF**) must be displayed outside or in the window.
- There is waiter service in all cafés, but you can drink at the bar or counter if you wish.
- When the bill is presented, the amount will be inclusive of service and VAT (**BTW**). Tipping: some additional small change is often given.
- Cafés serve both non-alcoholic drinks and alcoholic drinks and are normally open all day. Cream/milk is always served separately when ordering coffee or tea.
- Children are allowed into bars

WHAT TO SAY

I'll have . . . please	**Ik wil graag . . . alstublieft** ik wil hrahk . . . uls-too-bleeft
a cup of coffee	**een kop koffie** en kop koffee
a cup of tea	**een kop thee** en kop tay
with milk	**met melk** met melk
with lemon	**met citroen** met citroon
a glass of milk	**een glas melk** en hlus melk
a hot chocolate	**een kop chocolade** en kop shocolah-der
a chilled chocolate	**een glas chocomel** en hlus shoco-mel
a mineral water	**een mineral water** en meenerahl wah-ter
a lemonade	**een citroen limonade** en citroon leemo-nah-der
an orangeade	**een sinaasappel limonade** en seenahs-uppel leemo-nah-der
a Coca-Cola	**een Coca-Cola** en coca-cola
a fresh orange juice	**een sinaasappelsap** en seenahs-uppel-sup
a blackcurrant drink	**een cassis** en cussis
an apple juice	**een appelsap** en uppel-sup
a Pilsener beer (light ale)	**een Pils** en pils
a brown ale	**een donker bier** en donker beer
a bitter	**een bitter** en bitter
a draught beer	**een bier van het vat** en beer vun et vut

A glass of . . .	Een glas . . .
	een hlus . . .
Two glasses of . . .	Twee glazen . . .
	tway hlahzen . . .
red wine	rode wijn
	roder weyn
white wine	witte wijn
	witter weyn
rosé	rosé
	roh-say
dry	droog
	drohk
sweet	zoet
	zoot
A bottle of . . .	Een fles . . .
	en fles . . .
sparkling wine	mousserende wijn
	moossay-render weyn
champagne	champagne
	shum-pun-yer
A whisky . . .	Een whiskey . . .
	en wiskee . . .
with ice	met ijs
	met eys
with water	met water
	met wah-ter
with soda	met sodawater
	met soda-wah-ter
A gin . . .	Een gin/ginever . . .
	en gin/yer-nayver . . .
and tonic	met tonic
	met ton-nik
with lemon	met citroen
	met citroon
A brandy/cognac	Een cognac
	en con-yuc

The following are local drinks you may like to try:

een oude klare	a pure, mature Dutch gin
en *ow*der klah-rer	
advocaat	a brandy and egg liqueur with
ut-voh-k*ah*t	spices
bessenjenever	a red/blackcurrant gin liqueur
b*e*ssen-yer-n*a*y-ver	
kersen brandewijn	cherry brandy
k*ai*rsen br*u*nder-weyn	
citroen brandewijn	lemon brandy/gin (less sweet with
citr*oo*n br*u*nder-weyn	gin)
cognac grog	a hot diluted cognac with sugar
con-yuc hrok	and lemon slices
bisschop	a hot diluted red wine with orange
b*i*sskop	slices and spices

Other essential expressions:

Miss! [*This does not sound abrupt in Dutch*]	**Juffrouw!**
	yer-fr*ow*
Waiter!	**Ober!**
	ober
The bill, please	**De rekening, alstublieft**
	der r*a*yker-ning uls-too-bl*ee*ft
How much does that come to?	**Hoeveel is dat samen?**
	h*oo*-vale is dut s*a*h-men
Is service included?	**Is het inclusief?**
	is et in-cloo-s*ee*f
Where is the toilet, please?	**Waar is het toilet?**
	wahr is et twah-l*e*t

Ordering a snack

ESSENTIAL INFORMATION

- Look for any of these places:
  SNELBUFFET (refreshment bar)
  CAFETARIA (low-priced snacks available; service not included)
  VISWINKEL
  GEBAKKEN VIS] ready fried fish available
- Apart from snacks, the **cafetarias** and **snelbuffets** also sell canned or bottled beer, tea and coffee.
- In some regions mobile vans do hot snacks.
- If you want a sandwich lunch, look out for **KOFFIETAFEL**. You will be served a variety of breads, cold meats, cheeses – possibly a hot dish – and a bowl of soup or a salad. Coffee, milk or tea are also usually included.
- For cakes, see p. 64; for ice-creams, see p. 66; for picnic-type snacks, see p. 70.

WHAT TO SAY

I'll have . . . please	**Ik zou graag . . . hebben**
	ik zow hrahk . . . hebben
a cheese roll	**een broodje kaas**
	en brote-yer kahs
a ham roll	**een broodje ham**
	en brote-yer hum
a hamburger	**een hamburger**
	en humbur-her
an omelet	**een omelet**
	en omerlet
with mushrooms	**met champignons**
	met shum-peen-yons
with ham	**met ham**
	met hum
with cheese	**met kaas**
	met kahs

These are some other snacks you might like to try:

een boterham	an open sandwich
en boter-rum	

een dubbele boterham	a sandwich with two pieces of
en dub*ay*-lee b*o*ter-rum	bread, i.e. like our sandwiches
een croquet	a croquette
en croh-k*e*t	
een fricandel	a minced meat roll
en free-cun-d*e*l	
een saté	cubed meat (mostly pork or
en sateh	chicken) on skewers with a spicy
	peanut sauce
een pannekoek	a pancake
en p*u*nner-kook	
een saucijze broodje	a sausage roll
en sow-s*eyzer*-br*o*te-yer	
een broodje Tartaar	a minced beef (raw) roll
en br*o*te-yer tar-*tar*	
een tosti	a toastie (ham and cheese)
en tostee	
een uitsmijter	two slices of bread with ham, roast
en *o*-eet-smayter	beef or cheese, topped by two or
	three fried eggs
hutspot met klapstuk	carrots mashed with onions and
h*e*rts-pot met kl*u*p-sterk	potatoes, cooked with rib of pork
een kop erwtensoep	a cup of pea soup
en kop airten-soop	
een kop tomatensoep	a cup of tomato soup
en kop toh-m*ah*ten-soop	
een kop groentesoep	a cup of vegetable soup
en kop hr*oo*nter-soop	

You may wish to add to your order:

with chips	**met frites**
	met frits
with potato salad	**met aardappelsla**
	met *a*r-duppel-slah
with bread	**met brood**
	met br*o*te
with mustard	**met mosterd**
	met m*o*stert
with ketchup	**met ketchup**
	met k*e*t-shup
with mayonnaise	**met mayonaise**
	met mah-yon-*ai*ser

[*For other essential expressions, see* 'Ordering a drink, p. 82]

In a restaurant

ESSENTIAL INFORMATION

- The place to ask for: **EEN RESTAURANT** [*see p. 20*]
- You can eat at the following places:
  RESTAURANT
  HOTEL-RESTAURANT
  STATIONS-RESTAURATIE
  MOTEL
  CAFÉ-RESTAURANT
- By law, the menus must be displayed outside or in the window – and that is the *only* way to judge if a place is right for your needs.
- Self-service restaurants are not unknown, but most places have waiter service.
- A service charge is always added to the bill. Tipping is therefore optional.
- Most restaurants have children's portions.
- Some 700 restaurants offer a *tourist menu* (three courses) at a set price throughout the Netherlands although the courses themselves will differ from region to region. Restaurants participating in this scheme display the sign shown on the right.
- Hot meals are served from 12.00 p.m. – 2.00 p.m. at lunchtime and from 6.00 p.m. – 9.00/10.00 p.m. at night. After that many restaurants offer snacks for latecomers (soups, sausages, salads etc.). Many cities have Indonesian restaurants, where you will find the best *rijsttafel* (lit. 'rice table') outside Indonesia. This speciality consists of nine to ten varying dishes of meats, vegetables, fruits.

WHAT TO SAY

May I book a table?	**Kan ik een tafel reserveren?**
	kun ik en *tah*-fel ray-ser-*vai*ren
I have booked a table	**Ik heb een tafel gereserveerd**
	ik hep en *tah*-fel he-ray-ser-*vai*rt
A table . . .	**Een tafel . . .**
	en *tah*-fel . . .
for one	**voor één persoon**
	vor ayn pair-*soh*n
for three	**voor drie personen**
	vor dree pair-*soh*nen
The à la carte menu, please	**Het à la carte menu, alstublieft**
	et ah la cart mer-*noo*
	uls-too-b*leeft*
The fixed-price menu	**Het vastgestelde menu**
	et v*ust*-her-stelder mer-*noo*
Today's special menu	**Het menu van de dag**
	et mer-*noo* vun der duk
The tourist menu	**Het touristen menu**
	et too-*ris*ten mer-*noo*
What is this, please?	**Wat is dit, alstublieft?**
[point to menu]	wut is dit uls-too-b*leeft*
The wine list	**De wijnlijst**
	der weyn-leyst
A glass of wine	**Een glas wijn**
	en hlus weyn
A half-bottle	**Een halve fles**
	en h*ul*ver fles
A bottle	**Een fles**
	en fles
A litre	**Een liter**
	en *lee*ter
Red/white/rosé/house wine	**Rode/witte/rosé/huis wijn**
	roder/witter/roh-say/ho-ees weyn
Some more bread, please	**Nog wat brood, alstublieft**
	nok wut *bro*te uls-too-b*leeft*
Some more wine	**Nog wat wijn**
	nok wut weyn
Some oil	**Een beetje olie**
	en *bayt*-yer *o*lee
Some vinegar	**Een beetje azijn**
	en *bayt*-yer ah-*zeyn*

Some salt	**Een beetje zout**
	en b*a*yt-yer zowt
Some pepper	**Een beetje peper**
	en b*a*yt-yer p*a*per
Some water	**Een beetje water**
	en b*a*yt-yer w*a*h-ter
How much does that come to?	**Hoeveel is dat?**
	h*oo*-vale is dut
Is service included?	**Is het inclusief bediening?**
	is et *in*-cloo-seef ber-d*ee*ning
Where is the toilet, please?	**Waar is het toilet?**
	wahr is et twah-l*e*t
Miss! [*This does not sound abrupt in Dutch*]	**Juffrouw!**
	yer-fr*o*w
Waiter!	**Ober!**
	*o*ber
The bill, please	**De rekening, alstublieft**
	der r*a*yker-ning uls-too-bl*ee*ft

Key words for courses, as seen on some menus

[*Ask this question if you want the waiter to remind you of the choice*]

What have you got in the way of . . .	**Wat voor . . . heeft u?**
	wut vor . . . hayft oo
STARTERS?	**VOORGERECHTEN**
	vor-her-r*e*kten
SOUP?	**SOEP**
	soop
EGG DISHES?	**EIERGERECHTEN**
	ey-er-her-r*e*kten
FISH?	**VIS**
	vis
MEAT?	**VLEES**
	vlays
GAME?	**WILD**
	wilt
FOWL?	**GEVOGELTE**
	her-*voh*-helter
VEGETABLES?	**GROENTE**
	hr*oo*nter
CHEESE?	**KAAS**
	kahs
FRUIT?	**FRUIT**
	fro-eet

ICE-CREAM?	**IJS**
	eys
DESSERT?	**DESSERT**
	des-*sairt*

UNDERSTANDING THE MENU

● You will find the names of the principal ingredients of most dishes
on these pages:

Starters p. 70	Fruit p. 72
Meat p. 76	Cheese p. 71
Fish p. 79	Ice-cream p. 66
Vegetables p. 74	Dessert p. 64

Used together with the following lists of cooking and menu terms,
they should help you decode the menu.

● These cooking and menu terms are for understanding – not for
speaking.

Cooking and menu terms

aangemaakt	dressed
aspic	aspic
bouillon	broth, clear soup
doorgebakken	well-done
gebakken	fried, baked
gebraden	roasted
gefileerd	filleted
gegarneerd	garnished
geglazeerd	glazed
gegratineerd	au gratin
gegrilleerd	grilled
gekookt	boiled
gekruid	spiced
gelardeerd	larded
gemarineerd	marinated
gemengd	mixed
gepaneerd	dressed with eggs and breadcrumbs
gepocheerd	poached
geraapt	grated
gerookt	smoked
geroosterd	toasted
gesmoord	braised
gestoomd	steamed
gevulde	filled

gezouten	salted
in gelei	jellied
jus	gravy
kaasgerechten	cheese dishes
koude schotels	cold dishes
pikant	savoury
puree	mashed
ragout	ragout
rauw	raw
room	cream
salade/sla	salad
saté/sateh	meat cubes on sticks with peanut sauce
slagroom	whipped cream (with sugar)
soufflé	soufflé
wild en gevogelte	game and poultry
zoet	sweet
zuur	sour

Further words to help you understand the menu

aalbessen; rode, witte, zwarte	currants; red, white, black
aalbessen gelei	currant jelly
artisjok	artichoke
asperge	asparagus
aubergines	aubergines
augurken	pickled gherkins
avocado	avocado
bami	Indonesian noodle dish with diced pork and often shrimps
blinde vinken	veal fillet, filled with spiced minced veal, fried in butter
bloemkool	cauliflower
boerenkool (stamppot)	kale (hotchpotch)
borst	breast
bruine bonensoep	brown bean soup
brussels lof met ham en kaas	chicory with ham and cheese (oven dish)
chantilly crème met kastanje puree	whipped cream with chestnut purée
chinese kool	chinese cabbage
compote	stewed fruit
doperwten	peas
duitse biefstuk	hamburger steak

eend	duck
fazant	pheasant
flensjes	very thin pancakes
fondue	fondue
gebakken aardappels	fried potatoes
gebakken ananas	fried pineapple
gehakt	minced meat
gewelde boter	creamed butter
haantje	young cock
haas	hare
hachée	braised steak with onions, spices and vinegar
jachtschotel	hot-pot
kalfsvlees	veal
kappertjes saus	caper sauce
kapucijners	marrowfat peas
karbonade	chops
kervel	chervil
kip (gebraden)	chicken (roasted)
kotelet	cutlet
koude schotels	cold dishes
leverworst	liver sausage
loempia	Indonesian deep-fried pancake, filled with bamboo shoots, meat and vegetables
nasi goreng	Indonesian spicy rice dish
ossestaart soep	oxtail soup
paprika (gevulde)	green/red peppers (stuffed)
peterselie	parsley
prei	leeks
reebout	haunch of venison
roerei	scrambled egg
rolmop	rolled-up pickled herring filled with onion
russische eieren	hard boiled eggs with mayonnaise and caper sauce
schildpadsoep	turtle soup
snijbonen	green beans
sperciebonen	french beans
spruitjes	sprouts
taugé soup	bean sprouts soup
tonijn	tuna fish
zuurkool met spek	sauerkraut with boiled bacon

Health

ESSENTIAL INFORMATION

- For details of reciprocal health agreements between the UK and the Netherlands or Belgium ask for leaflet SA 30 at your local Department of Health and Social Security a month before leaving, or ask at your travel agent.
- In addition, it is preferable to purchase a medical insurance policy through the travel agent, a broker or a motoring organization.
- Take your own 'first line' first aid kit with you.
- For minor disorders and treatment at a chemist's, see p. 42.
- For finding your own way to a doctor, dentist, chemist or Health and Social Security Office (for reimbursement), see p. 20.
- The cost of the medical care of the tourist must be settled directly with the doctor, chemist, dentist, hospital, etc.
- Once in the Netherlands decide a definite plan of action in case of serious illness: communicate your problem to a near neighbour, the receptionist or someone you see regularly. You are then dependent on that person helping you obtain treatment.
- The name of the medical practitioner on duty at weekends and nights can be found in the local papers.

What's the matter?

I have a pain . . .	Ik heb pijn . . . .
	ik hep pain . . .
in my ankle	aan mijn enkel
	ahn mane enkel
in my arm	aan mijn arm
	ahn mane arm
in my back	in mijn rug
	in mane rerk
in my belly/tummy	in mijn buik
	in mane bo-eek
in my bowels	in mijn ingewanden
	in mane in-her-wunden
in my breast/chest	in mijn borst
	in mane borst

in my ear	**in mijn oor**
	in mane or
in my eyes	**in mijn oog**
	in mane *oak*
in my foot	**aan mijn voet**
	ahn mane voot
in my head	**in mijn hoofd**
	in mane hohft
in my heel	**aan mijn hiel**
	ahn mane heel
in my jaw	**aan mijn kaak**
	ahn mane kahk
in my leg	**in mijn been**
	in mane bane
in my neck	**in mijn hals**
	in mane huls
in my penis	**aan mijn penis**
	ahn mane p*ay*-nis
in my shoulder	**in mijn schouder**
	in mane sk*ow*der
in my stomach/abdomen	**in mijn maag**
	in mane mahk
in my testicle	**in mijn testikel**
	in mane t*e*stee-kel
in my throat	**in mijn keel**
	in mane kale
in my vagina	**in mijn vagina**
	in mane vah-h*ee*-nah
in my wrist	**aan mijn pols**
	ahn mane pols
I have a pain here *[point]*	**Ik heb hier pijn**
	ik hep here pain
I have toothache	**Ik heb kiespijn**
	ik hep k*ee*s-pain
I have broken ...	**Ik heb ... gebroken**
	ik hep ... herbr*o*ken
my dentures	**mijn kunstgebit**
	mane koonst-her-bit
my glasses	**mijn bril**
	mane bril

I have lost . . .	Ik heb . . . verloren
	ik hep . . . ver-loren
my contact lenses	mijn contact lenzen
	mane contuct lenzen
a filling	een vulling
	en verling
My child is ill	Mijn kind is ziek
	mane kint is zeek
He/she has a pain in	Hij/zij heeft pijn in zijn/haar . . .
his/her . . .	hey/zey hayft pain in zane/har . . .
ankle [see list above]	enkel
	enkel

How bad is it?

I'm ill	Ik ben ziek
	ik ben zeek
It is urgent	Het is dringend
	et is dring-ent
It's serious	Het is ernstig
	et is airn-stik
It's not serious	Het is niet ernstig
	et is neet airn-stik
It hurts	Het doet pijn
	et doot pain
It hurts a lot	Het doet erg pijn
	et doot airk pain
It doesn't hurt much	Het doet niet erg pijn
	et doot neet airk pain
The pain occurs . . .	De pijn komt . . .
	der pain komt . . .
every quarter of an hour	elk kwartier
	elk kwarteer
every half-hour	elk half uur
	elk hulf oor
every hour	elk uur
	elk oor
every day	elke dag
	elker duk

I have had it for . . .	**Ik heb het al . . .**
	ik hep et ul . . .
one hour/one day	**één uur/één dag**
	ayn oor/ayn duk
two hours/two days	**twee uur/twee dagen**
	tway oor/tway d*ah*-hen
It's a . . .	**Het is een . . .**
	et is en . . .
sharp pain	**scherpe pijn**
	sk*ai*rper pain
dull ache	**doffe pijn**
	d*o*ffer pain
nagging pain	**zeurende pijn**
	z*er*-render pain
I feel . . .	**Ik voel me . . .**
	ik vool mer . . .
dizzy	**duizelig**
	d*o*-ee-zer-lik
sick	**misselijk**
	m*i*sser-lik
weak	**slap**
	slup
feverish	**koortsig**
	k*o*rtsik

Already under treatment for something else?

I take . . . regularly [*show*]	**Ik neem geregeld . . .**
	ik name her-r*a*y-helt . . .
this medicine	**dit medicijn**
	dit may-dee-s*ey*n
these pills	**deze pillen**
	d*a*zer p*i*llen
I have . . .	**Ik heb . . .**
	ik hep . . .
a heart condition	**een hart conditie**
	en hart con-d*ee*-tsee
haemorrhoids	**aambeien**
	*ah*m-bey-yen
rheumatism	**reumatiek**
	rer-mah-t*ee*k

I think I have . . .	**Ik geloof dat ik . . . heb**
	ik her-*lohf* duk ik . . . hep
food poisoning	**voedselvergiftiging**
	vootsel-ver-hiftee-hing
sunstroke	**een zonnesteak**
	en *zo*nner-stake
I'm . . .	**Ik lijd aan . . .**
	ik leyt ahn . . .
diabetic	**diabetes**
	dee-ah-*bay*-tes
asthmatic	**asthma**
	*u*st-mah
I'm pregnant	**Ik ben zwanger**
	ik ben zw*u*ng-er
I'm allergic to penicillin	**Ik ben gevoelig voor penicilline**
	ik ben her-voolik vor penicill*ee*ner

Other essential expressions

Please can you help?	**Kunt u alstublieft helpen?**
	koont oo uls-too-bl*ee*ft *h*elpen
A doctor, please	**Een dokter, alstublieft**
	en *do*kter uls-too-bl*ee*ft
A dentist	**Een tandarts**
	en t*u*nt-arts
I don't speak Dutch	**Ik spreek geen nederlands**
	ik sprake hayn *n*ay-der-lunts
What time does . . . arrive?	**Hoe laat komt . . .**
	hoo laht komt . . .
the doctor	**de dokter?**
	der *do*kter
the dentist	**de tandarts?**
	der t*u*nt-arts

From the doctor: key sentences to understand:

Take this . . .	**Neem dit . . .** name dit . . .
every day/hour	**elke dag/uur** *e*lker duk/oor
four times a day	**vier maal per dag** veer mahl pair duk
Stay in bed	**Blijf in bed** bleyf in bet
Don't travel . . .	**Niet reizen . . .** neet r*e*yzen . . .
for . . . days/weeks	**voor . . . dagen/weken** vor . . . d*ah*-hen/w*a*ken
You must go to hospital	**U moet naar het ziekenhuis** oo moot nar et z*ee*ken-h*o*-ees

Problems: complaints, loss, theft

ESSENTIAL INFORMATION

- Problems with:
  camping facilities, see p. 36
  household appliances, see p. 54
  health, see p. 94
  the car, see p. 110
- If the worst comes to the worst, find a police station.
  To ask the way, see p. 20.
- Look for:
  POLITIE
- If you lose your passport, report the loss to the nearest police station and go to the British Consulate.

COMPLAINTS

I bought this . . .	**Ik kocht dit . . .** ik kokt dit . . .
today	**vandaag** vun-*dahk*
yesterday	**gisteren** *h*ister-ren
on Monday [*see p. 133*]	**maandag** m*ahn*-duk
It's no good	**Het is niet goed** et is neet hoot
Look	**Kijk** keyk
Here [*point*]	**Hier** here
Can you . . .	**Kunt u . . .** koont oo . . .
change it?	**het ruilen?** et r*o*-ee-len
mend it?	**het repareren?** et ray-pah-*ray*-ren
Here's the receipt	**Hier is de bon** here is der bon
Can I have a refund?	**Mag ik terugbetaling?** muk ik ter-*ruk*-ber-tahling
Can I see the manager?	**Mag ik de chef spreken?** muk ik der shef spr*ay*ken

LOSS
[*See also 'Theft' below: the lists are interchangeable*]

I have lost . . .	**Ik heb . . . verloren** ik hep . . . verl*o*ren
my bag	**mijn tas** mane tus
my bracelet	**mijn armband** mane *arm*-bunt
my camera	**mijn camera** mane *cah*mer-rah
my car keys	**mijn autosleutels** mane *ow*to-slertels

I have lost ...	**Ik heb ... verloren**
	ik hep ... verloren
my car logbook	**mijn auto papieren**
	mane *ow*to pah-*pee*-ren
my driving licence	**mijn rijbewijs**
	mane *rey*-ber-weys
my insurance certificate	**mijn verzekeringsbewijs**
	mane ver-*zay*kerrings-ber-weys
my jewellery	**mijn juwelen**
	mane yoo-*way*len
everything!	**alles!**
	ull-es

THEFT
[See also 'Loss' above: the lists are interchangeable]

Someone has stolen ...	**Iemand heeft ... gestolen**
	ee-munt hayft ... her-st*o*len
my car	**mijn auto**
	mane *ow*-to
my car radio	**mijn autoradio**
	mane *ow*to-rahdio
my keys	**mijn sleutels**
	mane sl*er*tels
my money	**mijn geld**
	mane helt
my necklace	**mijn ketting**
	mane ketting
my passport	**mijn paspoort**
	mane p*u*sport
my purse	**mijn portemonnaie**
	mane porter-mon*ay*
my radio	**mijn radio**
	mane *rah*dio
my tickets	**mijn kaartjes**
	mane k*art*-yers
my travellers' cheques	**mijn reischeques**
	mane *reys*-sheks
my wallet	**mijn portefeuille**
	mane porter-f*oy*-yer
my watch	**mijn horloge**
	mane hor-*loh*-sher
my luggage	**mijn bagage**
	mane bah-*hah*-sher

LIKELY REACTIONS: key words to understand

Wait	**Wacht**
	wukt
When?	**Wanneer?**
	wun-nair
Where?	**Waar?**
	wahr
Name?	**Naam?**
	nahm
Address?	**Adres?**
	ah-dres
I can't help you	**Ik kan u niet helpen**
	ik kun oo neet helpen
Nothing to do with me	**Dat is mijn zaak niet**
	dut is mane zahk neet

The post office

ESSENTIAL INFORMATION

- To find a post office, see p. 20.
- Key words to look for:
  POSTKANTOOR
  POSTERIJEN
  POST EN SPAARBANK
- Look for the following sign:

- For stamps look for the word **POSTZEGELS** on a machine, or **ZEGELVERKOOP** or **FRANKEERZEGELS** at a post office counter.
- Stamps may be obtained at a stationer's, provided postcards are also bought there.
- Stamp machines are yellow and red and contain the correct stamps for letters to EEC countries.
- Letter boxes are red and grey for twin boxes; others are red.
- For poste restante you should show your passport at the correct counter; a small fee is usually payable.

WHAT TO SAY

To England, please	**Naar Engeland, alstublieft** nar *eng*-er-lunt uls-too-bl*ee*ft

[Hand letters, cards or parcels over the counter]

To Australia	**Naar Australië** nar ah-oostr*ah*-lee-yer
To the United States	**Naar de Verenigde Staten** nar der ver-*ay*-nik-der st*ah*-ten

[For other countries, see p. 138]

How much is . . .	**Hoeveel is . . .** h*oo*-vale is . . .
this parcel (to Canada)?	**dit pakje (naar Canada)?** dit p*u*k-yer (nar c*ah*nada)
a letter (to New Zealand)?	**een brief (naar Nieuw Zeeland)?** en breef (nar new-z*ay*-lunt)
a postcard (to England)?	**een briefkaart (naar Engeland)?** en breef-kart (nar *eng*-er-lunt)
Airmail	**Luchtpost** l*er*kt-posst
Surface mail	**Zeepost** z*ay*-posst
One stamp, please	**Eén postzegel, alstublieft** ayn p*os*-say-hel uls-too-bl*ee*ft
Two stamps	**Twee postzegels** tway p*os*-say-hels
One (60) cent stamp	**Eén postzegel van (zestig) cent** ayn p*os*-say-hel vun (zestik) cent
I'd like to send a telegram	**Ik zou graag een telegram sturen** ik zow hrahk en telehr*um* st*oo*-ren

Telephoning

ESSENTIAL INFORMATION

- Unless you read and speak Dutch well, it is best not to make phone calls by yourself. Go to a post office and write the town and number you want on a piece of paper. Add **persoonlijk gesprek** if you want a person-to-person call or **BO** if you want to reverse the charges.
- Public telephones, **TELEFOON**, are mainly glass with blue frames.
- Instructions on how to use the phone are printed inside in several languages.
- The code for the UK is 0944, and for the USA 091; then dial the number you want (less any initial 0).
- You can ask at your local post office for a brochure on phoning England from abroad.
- To ask the way to a public telephone or post office, see p. 20.

WHAT TO SAY

Where can I make a telephone call?	**Waar kan ik telefoneren?**
	wahr kun ik telefon*ay*-ren
Local/abroad	**Lokaal/buitenland**
	*lo*kahl/b*o*-ee-ten-lunt
I'd like this number . . .	**Ik wou dit nummer . . .**
[*show number*]	ik wow dit n*oo*mmer . . .
in England	**in Engeland**
	in *e*ng-er-lunt
in Canada	**in Canada**
	in c*a*hnada
in the USA	**in de Verenigde Staten**
[*For other countries, see p. 138*]	in der ver-*ay*-nik-der st*a*h-ten
Can you dial it for me, please?	**Kunt u het voor me draaien, alstublieft?**
	koont oo et vor mer dr*a*h-yen uls-too-bl*ee*ft
How much is it?	**Hoeveel is het?**
	h*oo*-vale is et

Hello!	**Hallo!** hullo
May I speak to . . .?	**Mag ik met . . . spreken?** muk ik met . . . spr*ay*ken
Extension . . .	**Toestel . . .** too-st*e*l . . .
I'm sorry, I don't speak Dutch	**Het spijt me, ik spreek geen Nederlands** et sp*ate* mer ik spr*a*ke hayn n*ay*-der-lunts
Do you speak English?	**Spreekt u engels?** spr*ay*kt oo *e*ng-els
Thank you, I'll phone back	**Dank u, ik bel terug** dunk oo ik bel ter-*rer*k
Good-bye	**Daag** dahk

LIKELY REACTIONS

That's (4.50 guilders)	**Dat is (vier gulden vijftig)** dut is (v*ee*r h*oo*lden v*eyf*tik)
Cabin number (3)	**Cabine nummer (drie)** kah-b*ee*ner n*oo*mmer (dree)

[For numbers, see p. 129]

Don't hang up	**Niet ophangen** neet *o*p-hung-en
I'm trying to connect you	**Ik probeer u te verbinden** ik probeer oo ter ver-b*i*n-den
You're through	**U bent verbonden** oo bent ver-b*o*nden
There's a delay	**Er is vertraging** er is ver-tr*ah*-hing
I'll try again	**Ik zal het nog eens proberen** ik zul et n*o*k ayns prob*ay*-ren

Changing cheques and money

ESSENTIAL INFORMATION

- Finding your way to a bank or change bureau, see p. 20.
- Look for these words or signs on buildings:
  BANK (bank)
  GRENSWISSELKANTOREN NV
  (more commonly given as **GWK**: these are to be found in stations and at the borders only)
  BUREAU DE CHANGE
- Banks are open weekdays 9.00 a.m. – 4.00 p.m. The exchange offices (**WISSELKANTOREN**) are open Monday to Saturday and often in the evenings and on Sundays.
- To cash your own cheques, exactly as at home, use your banker's card where you see the Eurocheque sign. Write in English, in pounds.
- Exchange rate information might show the pound as:
  £, LONDEN, ENGELAND (GR BR) or the British flag.
- Have your passport ready.

WHAT TO SAY

I'd like to cash . . .	**Ik wou . . . wisselen** ik wow . . . *wi*sselen
this travellers' cheque	**deze reischeque** d*a*zer reys-shek
these travellers' cheques	**deze reischeques** d*a*zer reys-sheks
this cheque	**deze cheque** d*a*zer shek
I'd like to change this into guilders	**Ik wou dit graag omwisselen in guldens** ik wow dit hrahk *o*m-wisselen in h*oo*ldens
Here's . . .	**Hier is . . .** here is . . .
my banker's card	**mijn cheque kaart** mane sh*e*k kart
my passport	**mijn paspoort** mane p*u*sport

For excursions into neighbouring countries

I'd like to change this . . .　**Ik wou dit graag omwisselen . . .**
　[*show banknotes*]　ik wow dit hrahk om-wisselen . . .
　　into Belgian francs　**in belgische franken**
　　　in bel-hee-ser frunken
　　into French francs　**in franse franken**
　　　in frun-ser frunken
　　into German marks　**in duitse marken**
　　　in do-eet-ser marken

What is the rate of exchange?　**Wat is de koers?**
　　wut is der koors

LIKELY REACTIONS

Passport, please　**Paspoort, alstublieft**
　pusport uls-too-bleeft

Sign here　**Hier tekenen**
　here taker-nen

Your banker's card, please　**Uw cheque kaart, alstublieft**
　oo shek kart uls-too-bleeft

Go to the cash desk　**Naar de kassa, alstublieft**
　nar der kussa, uls-too-bleeft

Car travel

ESSENTIAL INFORMATION

- Finding a filling station or garage, see p. 20.
  Is it a self-service station? Look out for: **ZELFBEDIENING**
  Grades of petrol:
  NORMAAL (standard)
  SUPER (premium)
  DIESEL OLIE (diesel)
- 1 gallon is about 4½ litres (accurate enough for up to 6 gallons).
- The minimum sale is often 5 litres (less at self-service pumps).
- Filling stations may be able to deal with minor mechanical problems during the day only. For major repairs you have to go to a garage.
- All main roads are patrolled by the yellow cars of the Royal Dutch Touring Club (**ANWB**) between 7.00 a.m. and 12.00 p.m. Telephones have been installed along Holland's main roads to be used to obtain information from the local **ANWB** station. They will assist tourists whose cars break down. If you are not a member of an automobile club affiliated with the **AIT**, roadside service will be available if you become a temporary member of the **ANWB**.
- Unfamiliar road signs and warnings, see p. 125.

WHAT TO SAY
[*For numbers, see p. 129*]

(Nine) litres of . . .	**(Negen) liter . . .** (n*ay*hen) l*ee*ter . . .
(20) guilders of . . .	**Voor (twintig) gulden . . .** vor (twintik) h*oo*lden . . .
Fill it up, please	**Vol alstublieft** vol uls-too-bl*ee*ft
standard	**normaal** norm*ah*l
premium	**super** s*oo*per
diesel	**diesel** diesel

Will you check . . .	**Wilt u . . . nakijken?**
	wilt oo . . . n*ah*-kayken
the oil?	**de olie**
	der *o*lee
the battery?	**de accu**
	der *u*ccoo
the radiator?	**de radiator**
	der rah-d*ee*-ah-to*r*
the tyres?	**de banden**
	der b*u*nden
I have run out of petrol	**Ik zit zonder benzine**
	ik zit z*o*nder ben-z*ee*ne*r*
Can I borrow a can, please?	**Kan ik een blik lenen,**
	alstublieft?
	k*u*n ik en blik l*ay*-nen,
	uls-too-bl*ee*ft
My car has broken down	**Ik heb auto-pech**
	ik hep *ow*to-pek
My car won't start	**Mijn auto wil niet starten**
	mane *ow*to wil neet st*a*rten
I've had an accident	**Ik heb een ongeluk gehad**
	ik hep en *o*n-her-luk her-h*u*t
I've lost my car keys	**Ik heb mijn autosleutels verloren**
	ik hep mane *ow*to-slertels
	ver-l*o*ren
My car is . . .	**Mijn auto is . . .**
	mane *ow*to is . . .
two kilometres away	**twee kilometer hier vandaan**
	tway k*i*lo-may-ter here vun-d*ah*n
three kilometres away	**drie kilometer hier vandaan**
	dree k*i*lo-may-ter here vun-d*ah*n
Can you help me, please?	**Kunt u me helpen, alstublieft?**
	koont oo mer h*e*lpen uls-too-bl*ee*ft
Do you do repairs?	**Doet u reparaties?**
	doot oo ray-pah-r*ah*tsees
I have a puncture	**Ik heb een lekke band**
	ik hep en l*e*kker b*u*nt
I have a broken windscreen	**Ik heb een kapotte voorruit**
	ik hep en kah-p*o*tter vor-ro-eet
I think the problem is here . . . [*point*]	**Ik denk dat het probleem hier is . . .**
	ik denk dut et pro-bl*a*me here is . . .

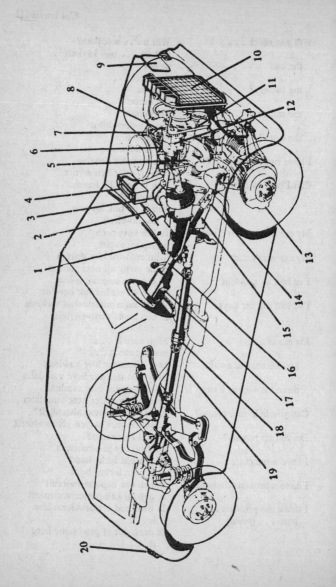

1	windscreen wipers	ruitenwissers	ro-ee-ten-wissers
2	fuses	zekeringen	zayker-ringen
3	heater	verwarming	ver-ahr-ming
4	battery	accu	uccoo
5	engine	motor	motor
6	fuel pump	benzinepomp	ben-zeener-pomp
7	starter motor	startmotor	start-mo-tor
8	carburettor	carburateur	car-boo-rah-ter
9	lights	lampen	lumpen
10	radiator	radiator	rah-dee-ah-tor

11	fan belt	ventilator-riem	ven-tee-lah-tor-reem
12	generator	dynamo	deena-mo
13	brakes	remmen	remmen
14	clutch	koppeling	kopper-ling
15	gear box	schakeldoos	skahkel-dose
16	steering	stuurinrichting	stoor-in-rikting
17	ignition	ontsteker	on-staker
18	transmission	transmissie	truns-mis-see
19	exhaust	uitlaat	o-eet-laht
20	indicators	richtingaanwijzers	rikting-ahn-weyzers

I don't know what is wrong
Ik weet niet wat het is
ik wate neet wut et is

Can you . . .
Kunt u . . .
koont oo . . .

  repair the fault?
de fout herstellen?
der fowt h*air*-stellen

  come and look?
eens kijken?
ayns k*ay*ken

  estimate the cost?
de kosten schatten?
der k*o*sten sk*u*tten

  write it down?
het opschrijven?
et *o*p-skrayven

Do you accept these coupons?
Accepteert u deze bonnen?
uccep-tairt oo d*a*zer b*o*nnen

How long will the repairs take?
Hoelang duurt de reparatie?
h*oo*-lung doort der ray-pah-r*ah*tsee

When will the car be ready?
Wanneer is de auto klaar?
wunnair is der *ow*to klar

Can I see the bill?
Mag ik de rekening zien?
muk ik der r*a*ker-ning zeen

This is my insurance document
Dit is mijn verzekeringsbewijs
dit is mane ver-z*a*ker-rings-ber-weys

HIRING A CAR

Can I hire a car?
Kan ik een auto huren?
kun ik en *ow*to h*oo*-ren

I need a car . . .
Ik heb een auto nodig . . .
ik hep en *ow*to n*o*dik . . .

  for two people
voor twee personen
vor tway pair-s*oh*nen

  for five people
voor vijf personen
vor veyf pair-s*oh*nen

  for one day
voor één dag
vor ayn duk

  for five days
voor vijf dagen
vor veyf d*ah*-hen

  for a week
voor één week
vor ayn wake

Can you write down . . . | **Kunt u opschrijven . . .**
| koont oo *op*-skray-ven . . .
the deposit to pay? | **de vooruit te betalen som?**
| der vor-*o*-eet ter ber-*tah*len som
the charge per kilometre? | **de prijs per kilometer?**
| der preys pair k*i*lo-may-ter
the daily charge? | **de prijs per dag?**
| der preys pair duk
the cost of insurance | **de verzekeringskosten?**
| der ver-*zaker*-rings-kos-ten
Can I leave it in (Edam)? | **Kan ik de auto in (Edam) achterlaten?**
| kun ik der *ow*to in (*ay*-dam) *u*kter-lah-ten
What documents do I need? | **Welke papieren heb ik nodig?**
| *we*lker pah-*pee*-ren hep ik n*o*dik

LIKELY REACTIONS

I don't do repairs | **Ik repareer niet**
| ik ray-pah-r*ai*r neet
Where is your car? | **Waar is uw auto?**
| wahr is oo *ow*to
What make is it? | **Welk merk is het?**
| welk mairk is et
Come back tomorrow/on Wednesday [*For days of the week, see p. 133*] | **Kom morgen/woensdag terug**
| kom mor-hen/w*oo*ns-duk ter-r*er*k
We don't hire cars | **Wij verhuren geen auto's**
| way ver-h*oo*ren hayn *ow*tos
Your driving licence, please? | **Uw rijbewijs, alstublieft?**
| oo r*ey*-ber-weys uls-too-bl*ee*ft
The mileage is unlimited | **Het kilometerverbruik is onbeperkt**
| et k*i*lomay-ter-ver-bro-eek is on-ber-p*ai*rkt

Public transport

ESSENTIAL INFORMATION

- Finding the way to the bus station, a bus, a tram stop, the railway station and a taxi rank, see p. 20.
- Remember that queuing for buses is unheard of!
- It is less usual to hail a taxi in the street: go instead to a taxi rank or telephone a taxi firm.
- These are the different types of trains, graded according to speed (fastest to slowest):
  TEE (Trans-Europa Express)
  INTERCITY NETWORK (national system of fast trains stopping only at a few stations)
  STOPTREINEN (stopping at all stations)
  Key words on signs: [*see also p. 125*]
  TREINKAARTJES (tickets)
  LOKET (ticket office)
  INGANG (entrance)
  UITGANG (exit)
  VERBODEN (forbidden)
  PERRON (platform)
  DOORGAAND VERKEER (transit passengers)
  WACHTKAMER (waiting room)
  INLICHTINGEN (information)
  BAGAGE DEPOT (left luggage)
  AANKOMST (arrivals)
  VERTREK (departures)
  NS (initials of Dutch railways)
  BUSHALTE (bus stop)
  DIENSTREGELING (timetable)
- Buying a ticket: train tickets are available at the station ticket office, in some main post offices and in some tobacconists'.
- When travelling by bus or tram you usually pay as you enter. A bus and tram **STRIPPENKAART** can be bought at post offices.
- There is a 'rover ticket' allowing unlimited travel through Holland for 3–7 days.
- A **GROEP KAART** permits unlimited travel by train for 2–6 persons for one day at a reduced rate.
- In some towns you can purchase a tram ticket which allows you to interchange between trams in the one direction.

WHAT TO SAY

Where does the train for (Rotterdam) leave from?	**Van waar vertrekt de trein naar (Rotterdam)?**
	vun wahr ver-trekt der train nar (rotter-dum)
At what time does the train for (Rotterdam) leave?	**Hoe laat vertrekt de trein naar (Rotterdam)?**
	hoo laht ver-trekt der train nar (rotter-dum)
At what time does the train arrive in (Rotterdam)?	**Hoe laat komt de trein in (Rotterdam) aan?**
	hoo laht komt der train in (rotter-dum) ahn
Is this the train for (Rotterdam)?	**Is dit de trein naar (Rotterdam)?**
	is dit der train nar (rotter-dum)
Where does the bus for (Edam) leave from?	**Van waar vertrekt de bus naar (Edam)?**
	vun wahr ver-trekt der bus nar (ay-dum)
At what time does the bus leave for (Edam)?	**Hoe laat vertrekt de bus naar (Edam)?**
	hoo laat ver-trekt der bus nar (ay-dum)
At what time does the bus arrive at (Edam)?	**Hoe laat komt de bus in (Edam) aan?**
	hoo laht komt der bus in (ay-dum) ahn
Is this the bus for (Edam)?	**Is dit de bus naar (Edam)?**
	is dit der bus nar (ay-dum)
Do I have to change?	**Moet ik overstappen?**
	moot ik over-stuppen

Where does . . . leave from?	**Van waar vertrekt . . .**
	vun wahr ver-trekt . . .
the bus	**de bus?**
	der bus
the train	**de trein?**
	der train
the underground	**de metro?**
	der maytro
the boat/ferry	**de boot/de veerboot?**
	der boat/der vayr-boat
for the airport	**naar het vliegveld?**
	nar et vleek-velt
for the cathedral	**naar de cathedraal?**
	nar der kutter-drahl
for the beach	**naar het strand?**
	nar et strunt
for the market place	**naar de markt?**
	nar der markt
for the railway station	**naar het spoorwegstation?**
	nar et spor-wek-stat-see-on
for the town centre	**naar het stadscentrum?**
	nar et stuts-centrem
for the town hall	**naar het gemeentehuis?**
	nar et her-maynter-ho-ess
for the St Bavo church	**naar de Sint Bavo kerk?**
	nar der sint bahvoh kairk
for the swimming pool	**naar het zwembad?**
	nar et zwem-but
Is this . . .	**Is dit . . .**
	is dit . . .
the bus for the market place?	**de bus voor het marktplein?**
	der bus vor et markt-plain
the tram for the station?	**de tram voor het spoowegstation?**
	der trem vor et spor-wek-stat-see-on
Where can I get a taxi?	**Waar kan ik een taxi krijgen?**
	wahr kun ik en tuk-see kray-hen
Can you put me off at the right stop, please?	**Kunt u mij op de juiste plaats afzetten, alstublieft?**
	koont oo mey op der yo-ees-ter plahts uf-zetten uls-too-bleeft

Can I book a seat?	**Kan ik een plaats bespreken?**
	kun ik en plahts ber-sprayken
A single	**Een enkele**
	en enkerler
A return	**Een retour**
	en rer-toor
First class	**Eerste klas**
	airster klus
Second class	**Tweede klas**
	tway-der klus
One adult	**Eén volwassene**
	ayn vol-wusserner
Two adults	**Twee volwassenen**
	tway vol-wussernen
and one child	**en één kind**
	en ayn kint
and two children	**en twee kinderen**
	en tway kin-der-ren
How much is it?	**Hoeveel is het?**
	hoo-vale is et

LIKELY REACTIONS

Over there	**Daar**
	dar
Here	**Hier**
	here
Platform (1)	**(Eerste) perron**
	(airster) peron
At 16.00	**Om zestien ur**
[*For times, see p. 131*]	om zesteen oor
Change at (Dordrecht)	**In (Dordrecht) overstappen**
	in (dor-drekt) over-stuppen
Change at (the town hall)	**Bij het (Gemeentehuis) overstappen**
	bey et (her-maynter-ho-ees)
	over-stuppen
This is your stop	**Dit is uw halte**
	dit is oo hulter
There's only first class	**Er is alleen eerste klas**
	er is ul-layn airster klus
There's a supplement	**Er is toeslag op**
	er is too-sluk op

Leisure

ESSENTIAL INFORMATION

- Finding the way to a place of entertainment, see p. 20.
- For times of day, see p. 131.
- Important signs, see p. 125.
- At the seaside, beach chairs are for hire.
- No smoking in cinemas, theatres or concert halls, and in some restaurants.
- Cinemas always show films in the original language with Dutch subtitles.
- It is customary to leave one's coat in the cloakroom in theatres.

WHAT TO SAY

At what time does . . . open?	**Hoe laat opent . . .** *hoo*-laht *o*pent . . .
the art gallery	**de kunst galerij?** der koonst hah-ler-*rey*
the botanical garden	**de botanische tuin?** der boh-*tah*-nee-ser *to*-een
the cinema	**de bioscoop?** der bee-os-*cope*
the concert hall	**het concertgebouw?** et con-sairt-her-ba-*oo*
the disco	**de disco?** der *d*isco
the museum	**het museum?** et moo-s*ayem*
the night club	**de nacht club?** der nukt cloop
the sports stadium	**het stadion?** et st*ah*-dee-on
the swimming pool	**het zwembad?** et zwem-but
the theatre ·	**het theater?** et tay-*ah*-ter
the zoo	**de dierentuin?** der d*ee*-ren-t*o*-een

At what time does . . . close?	**Hoe laat sluit . . .**
	hoo-laht slo-eet . . .
the skating rink	**de ijsbaan?**
[see above list]	der eys-bahn
At what time does . . . start?	**Hoe laat begint . . .**
	hoo-laht ber-hint . . .
the cabaret	**het cabaret?**
	et cah-bah-ret
the concert	**het concert?**
	et con-sairt
the film	**de film?**
	der film
the match	**de wedstrijd?**
	der wet-strait
the play	**het toneelstuk?**
	et toh-nayl-sterk
the race	**de race?**
	der race
How much is it . . .	**Hoeveel is het . . .**
	hoo-vale is et . . .
for an adult?	**voor een volwassene?**
	vor ayn vol-wusserner
for a child?	**voor een kind?**
	vor en kint
Two adults, please	**Twee volwassenen, alstublieft**
	tway vol-wussernen uls-too-bleeft
Three children, please	**Drie kinderen, alstublieft**
[state price, if there is a choice]	dree kin-der-ren uls-too-bleeft
Stalls/circle	**Stalles/arena**
	stul-les/ah-ray-na
Do you have . . .	**Heeft u . . .**
	heyft oo . . .
a programme?	**een programma?**
	en proh-hrumma
a guide book?	**een gids?**
	en hits
Where's the toilet, please?	**Waar is het toilet, alstublieft?**
	wahr is et twah-let uls-too-bleeft
Where's the cloakroom?	**Waar is de garderobe?**
	wahr is der harder-rober

I would like lessons in . . .	**Ik wou les hebben in . . .**
	ik wow les hebben in . . .
sailing	**zeilen**
	zaylen
skating	**schaatsen**
	skah-tsen
water skiing	**water skiën**
	wah-ter skee-yen
Can I hire . . .	**Kan ik . . . huren?**
	kun ik . . . hoo-ren
a boat?	**een boot**
	en boat
a fishing rod?	**een hengel**
	en heng-el
a deck chair?	**een dekstoel**
	en dek-stool
a parasol?	**een parasol**
	en pah-rah-sol
the necessary equipment?	**de benodigdheden**
	der ber-nodikt-hayden
How much is it . . .	**Hoeveel is het . . .**
	hoo-vale is et . . .
per day/per hour?	**per dag/per uur?**
	pair duk/pair oor
Do I need a licence?	**Heb ik een vergunning nodig?**
	hep ik en ver-hunning nodik

Asking if things are allowed

ESSENTIAL INFORMATION

- May one smoke here?
  May we smoke here?
  May I smoke here?
  Can one smoke here?   **Kan men hier roken?**
  Can we smoke here?
  Can I smoke here?
- All these English variations can be expressed in one way in Dutch.
  To save space, only the first English version (May one . . .?) is
  shown below.

WHAT TO SAY

Excuse me, please . . .	**Neem me niet kwalijk . . .**
	name mer neet kw*a*h-lek
May one . . .	**Kan men . . .**
	kun men . . .
camp here?	**hier kamperen?**
	here kum-p*a*y-ren
come in?	**binnen komen?**
	b*i*nnen k*o*h-men
dance here?	**hier dansen?**
	here d*u*n-sen
fish here?	**hier vissen?**
	here v*i*ssen
get a drink here?	**hier wat te drinken halen?**
	here wut ter dr*i*nken h*a*hlen
get out this way?	**hier door naar buiten gaan?**
	here dor nar b*o*-ee-ten hahn
leave one's things here?	**zijn spullen hier laten?**
	zane sp*e*rlen here l*a*hten
look around?	**hier rondkijken?**
	here r*o*nt-kayken
park here?	**hier parkeren?**
	here par-k*a*yren
picnic here?	**hier picknicken?**
	here p*i*cknicken

May one . . .	**Kan men . . .**
	kun men . . .
sit here?	**hier zitten?**
	here zitten
smoke here?	**hier roken?**
	here roken
swim here?	**hier zwemmen?**
	here zwemmen
telephone here?	**hier telefoneren?**
	here telefonay-ren
wait here?	**hier wachten?**
	here wukten

LIKELY REACTIONS

Yes, certainly	**Ja, zeker**
	yah zayker
Help yourself	**Gaat uw gang**
	haht oo hung
I think so	**Ik geloof het wel**
	ik her-lohf et wel
Of course	**Natuurlijk**
	nah-toor-lik
Yes, but be careful	**Ja, maar wees voorzichtig**
	yah mar ways vor-ziktik
No, certainly not	**Nee, beslist niet**
	nay ber-slist neet
I don't think so	**Ik geloof het niet**
	ik her-lohf et neet
Not normally	**Normaal niet**
	nor-mahl neet
Sorry	**Sorry**
	sorry

Reference

PUBLIC NOTICES

- Key words on signs for drivers, pedestrians, travellers, shoppers and overnight guests.

AANKOMST	Arrival
ALLEEN BUSSEN	Buses only
BADKAMER	Bathroom
BAGAGE DEPOT	Left luggage
BAR	Bar
BELLEN	Ring (bell)
BEZET	Occupied
BRANDWEER	Fire brigade
BUFFET	Buffet
BUSHALTE	Bus stop
DAMES	Ladies
DOORGAAND VERKEER	Through traffic
DOUANE	Customs
DOUCHE	Shower
DRINKWATER	Drinking water
DUWEN	Push
EHBO	First aid
EENRICHTING VERKEER	One way traffic
EETKAMER	Dining room
EINDE SNELWEG	End of motorway
FIETSERS OVERSTEKEN	Cyclists cross here
FIETSPAD	Cycle path
GA	Go
GEEN INGANG	No entrance
GEEN TOEGANG	No admission
GERESERVEERD	Reserved
GESLOTEN	Closed
GEVAARLIJKE BOCHT	Dangerous curve
GIDS	Guide
HALT	Stop
HEET	Hot
HEREN	Gentlemen
INGANG	Entrance
INHALEN VERBODEN	Overtaking forbidden
INLICHTINGEN	Information/inquiries

KAMERS TE HUUR	Rooms vacant
KASSA	Cash desk
KLOPPEN	Knock (on door)
KOUD	Cold
KRUISWEG	Crossroads/junction
LANGZAAM RIJDEN	Drive slowly
LEVENSGEVAARLIJK	Danger
LICHTEN AAN	Lights on
LIFT	Lift/elevator
METRO	Underground (railway/train)
NIET AANRAKEN	Do not touch
NIET BADEN/ZWEMMEN	No bathing/swimming
NIET PARKEREN	No parking
NIET ROKEN	No smoking
NOODUITGANG	Emergency exit
ONBEWAAKTE OVERWEG	Unguarded level crossing
ONGELUK	Accident
OPEN	Open
OPGELET (TREINEN)	Beware (trains)
OVERSTEKEN	Cross over
OVERTREDERS WORDEN GESTRAFT	Trespassers will be prosecuted
OVERWEG	Level crossing
PARKEERPLAATS	Parking place
PARKEERSCHIJF VERPLICHT	Parking discs obligatory
PARKEREN BEPERKT	Limited parking
PAS OP VOOR DE HOND	Beware of the dog
PERRON	Platform
PLAATSBEWIJZEN	Tickets
POLITIE	Police
PORTIER	Porter
PRIVÉ	Private
RECEPTIE	Reception
RECHTS HOUDEN	Keep right
RECHTS VOORRANG	Priority to the right
RESERVERINGEN	Reservations
RESTAURATIEWAGEN	Dining car
ROKEN TOEGESTAAN	Smoking permitted
ROLTRAP	Escalator
SCHOOL	School
SLAAPWAGEN	Sleeping car

SLECHT WEGDEK	Bad road surface
SLIP GEVAAR	Slippery road
SNELWEG	Motorway
SOUTERRAIN	Basement
SPECIALE AANBIEDING	Special offer
SPREEKUUR	Surgery hours
STAANPLAATSEN	Standing room
STEENSLAG	Loose chippings
STOP	Stop
TE HUUR	For hire
TE KOOP	For sale
TOL	Toll
TREKKEN	Pull
TWEE-RICHTING VERKEER	Two-way traffic
UIT	Out
UITGANG	Exit
UITVERKOOP	Sale
VERBODEN	Forbidden/prohibited
VERDIEPING: EERSTE/ TWEEDE/DERDE	Floor: first/ second/third
VERKEERSLICHTEN	Traffic lights
VERTREK	Departure
VIADUCT	Viaduct
VOETGANGERS	Pedestrians
VOOR ZWAAR VERKEER	For heavy traffic
VOORRANG VERLENEN	Give way
VOORRANGSWEG	Major road
VOORSORTEREN	Filter/get in lane
VRIJ	Vacant
VRIJE TOEGANG	Free entrance
WAARSCHUWING	Warning
WACHT!	Wait!
WACHTKAMER	Waiting room
WEG VERSMALLING	Road narrowing
WEGOMLEGGING	Diversion
WERK IN UITVOERING	Roadworks ahead
ZACHTE BERM	Soft verge
ZIEKENHUIS	Hospital

ABBREVIATIONS

ANWB	Algemene Nederlandse Wielrijders Bond	Royal Dutch Touring Club
aub	alstublieft	if you please
BTW	Bijzonder Toegevoegde Waarde	VAT
CS	Centraal Station	Central Station
cm	centimeter	centimetre
Dr	Doctor	doctor
enz	enzovoort	et cetera
Expo	Expositie	exposition
F/Fl	gulden	guilder
GWK	Grens Wisselkantoor	border exchange office
Hr	Heer	Mr
KLM	Koninklijke Nederlandse Luchtvaartmaatschappij	Royal Dutch Airlines
km	kilometer	kilometre
KNAC	Koninklijke Nederlandse Automobiel Club	Royal Dutch Automobile Association
kw	kilowatt	kilowatt
Mej	Mejuffrouw	Miss
m	meter	metre
M	Metro	underground train
Mevr Mw	Mevrouw	Mrs
med	medisch	medical
Ned/Nld	Nederland	the Netherlands
NS	Nederlandse Spoorwegen	Dutch Railways
NFN	Nederlandse Federatie van Naturalisme	Netherlands Federation of Naturalism
NJHC	Nederlandse Jeugd-herberg Centrale	Dutch Youth Hostel Organization
NNTB	Nederlands Nationaal Touristen Bureau	Netherlands National Tourist Office
NRC	Nederlands Reserveer Centrum	Netherlands (National) Reservation
Pol	Politie	police
Prov	Provincie	province
PTT	Post Telegraaf Telefoon	the Post Office
TV	Televisie	television
VVV	Vereniging Vreemdelingen Verkeer	tourist office
WW	Wegenwacht	Automobile Association
Z	Zelfbediening	Self-service
z	zuid	south

NUMBERS
Cardinal numbers

0	nul	nerl
1	één	ayn
2	twee	tway
3	drie	dree
4	vier	veer
5	vijf	veyf
6	zes	zes
7	zeven	zayven
8	acht	ukt
9	negen	nayhen
10	tien	teen
11	elf	elf
12	twaalf	twahlf
13	dertien	dairteen
14	veertien	vairteen
15	vijftien	veyfteen
16	zestien	zesteen
17	zeventien	zayventeen
18	achttien	ukteen
19	negentien	nayhenteen
20	twintig	twintik
21	éénentwintig	ayn-en-twintik
22	tweeëntwintig	tway-en-twintik
23	drieëntwintig	dree-en-twintik
24	vierentwintig	veer-en-twintik
25	vijfentwintig	veyf-en-twintik
26	zesentwintig	zes-en-twintik
27	zevenentwintig	zayven-en-twintik
28	achtentwintig	ukt-en-twintik
29	negenentwintig	nayhen-en-twintik
30	dertig	dairtik
31	éénendertig	ayn-en-dairtik
35	vijfendertig	veyf-en-dairtik
40	veertig	vairtik
41	éénenveertig	ayn-en-vairtik
50	vijftig	veyftik
51	éénenvijftig	ayn-en-veyftik
60	zestig	zestik
70	zeventig	zayventik
80	tachtig	tuktik
81	éénentachtig	ayn-én-tuktik

90	negentig	nayhentik
95	vijfennegentig	veyf-en-nayhentik
100	honderd	hondert
101	honderdéén	hondert-ayn
102	honderdtwee	hondert-tway
125	hondervijfentwintig	hondert-veyf-en-twintik
150	honderdvijftig	hondert-veyftik
175	hondervijfenzeventig	hondert-veyf-en-zayventik
200	tweehonderd	tway-hondert
300	driehonderd	dree-hondert
400	vierhonderd	veer-hondert
500	vijfhonderd	veyf-hondert
1000	duizend	do-ee-zent
1100	elfhonderd	elf-hondert
3000	drieduizend	dree-do-ee-zent
5000	vijfduizend	veyf-do-ee-zent
10,000	tienduizend	teen-do-ee-zent
100,000	honderdduizend	hondert-do-ee-zent
1,000,000	één miljoen	ayn mil-yoon

Ordinal numbers

1st	eerste	air-ster
2nd	tweede	tway-der
3rd	derde	dair-der
4th	vierde	veer-der
5th	vijfde	veyf-der
6th	zesde	zes-der
7th	zevende	zayven-der
8th	achtste	ukt-ster
9th	negende	nayhen-der
10th	tiende	teender
11th	elfde	elf-der
12th	twaalfde	twahlf-der

TIME

What time is it?	Hoe laat is het?
	hoo laht is et
It's ...	Het is ...
	et is ...
one o'clock	één uur
	ayn oor

two o'clock	**twee uur**
	tway oor
three o'clock	**drie uhr**
	dree oor
four o'clock	**vier uur**
	veer oor
in the morning	**'s morgens**
	sm*o*r-hens
in the afternoon	**'s middags**
	sm*i*d-ducks
in the evening	**'s avonds**
	s*ah*vents
at night	**'s nachts**
	snukts
It's . . .	**Het is . . .**
	et is . . .
noon	**middag**
	m*i*d-duk
midnight	**middernacht**
	midder-n*u*kt
It's . . .	**Het is . . .**
	et is . . .
five past five	**vijf over vijf**
	v*e*yf over v*e*yf
ten past five	**tien over vijf**
	teen *o*ver v*e*yf
a quarter past five	**kwart over vijf**
	kwart *o*ver v*e*yf
twenty past five	**twintig over vijf**
	tw*i*ntik *o*ver v*e*yf
twenty-five past five	**vijf vóór half zes**
	v*e*yf vor hulf zes
half past five	**half zes**
	hulf zes
twenty-five to six	**vijf over half zes**
	v*e*yf *o*ver hulf zes
twenty to six	**twintig vóór zes**
	tw*i*ntik voor zes
a quarter to six	**kwart vóór zes**
	kwart vor zes
ten to six	**tien vóór zes**
	teen vor zes
five to six	**vijf vóór zes**
	v*e*yf vor zes

At what time . . . (does the train leave)?	Hoe laat . . . (vertrekt de trein)? hoo laht . . . (ver-trekt der train)
At . . .	Om . . . om . . .
13.00	**dertien uur** dair-teen oor
14.05	**veertien uur vijf** vairteen uur veyf
15.10	**vijftien uur tien** veyfteen oor teen
16.15	**zestien uur vijftien** zesteen oor veyfteen
17.20	**zeventien uur twintig** zayventeen oor twintik
18.25	**achttien uur vijfentwintig** ukteen oor veyf-en-twintik
19.30	**negentien uur dertig** nayhenteen oor dairtik
20.35	**twintig uur vijfendertig** twintik oor veyf-en-dairtik
21.40	**éénentwintig uur veerig** ayn-en-twintik oor veertik
22.45	**tweeëntwintig uur vijfenveertig** tway-en-twin-tik oor veyf-en-vairtik
23.50	**drieëntwintig uur vijftig** dree-en-twintik oor veyftik
0.55	**vijf minuten vóór één** veyf mee-nooten vor ayn
in ten minutes	**binnen tien minuten** binnen teen mee-nooten
In a quarter of an hour	**binnen een kwartier** binnen en kwar-teer
in half an hour	**binnen een half uur** binnen en hulf oor
in three-quarters of an hour	**binnen drie kwartier** binnen dree kwar-teer

DAYS

Monday	**maandag**
	mahn-duk
Tuesday	**dinsdag**
	dins-duk
Wednesday	**woensdag**
	woons-duk
Thursday	**donderdag**
	donder-duk
Friday	**vrijdag**
	vrey-duk
Saturday	**zaterdag**
	zahter-duk
Sunday	**zondag**
	zon-duk
last Monday	**verleden maandag**
	ver-layden mahn-duk
next Tuesday	**aanstaande dinsdag**
	ahn-stahn-der dins-duk
on Wednesday	**op woensdag**
	op woons-duk
on Thursdays	**op donderdag**
	op donder-duk
until Friday	**tot vrijdag**
	tot vrey-duk
before Saturday	**vóór zaterdag**
	vor zahter-duk
after Sunday	**na zondag**
	na zon-duk
the day before yesterday	**eergisteren**
	air-histeren
two days ago	**twee dagen geleden**
	tway dah-hen her-laden
yesterday	**gisteren**
	histeren
yesterday morning	**gisterenmorgen**
	histeren-mor-hen
yesterday afternoon	**gisterenmiddag**
	histeren-mid-duk
last night	**gisterenavond**
	histeren-ahvent
today	**vandaag**
	vun-dahk

this morning	**vanmorgen** vun-mor-hen
this afternoon	**vanmiddag** vun-mid-duk
tonight	**vanavond** vun-ahvent
tomorrow	**morgen** mor-hen
tomorrow morning	**morgenochtend** mor-hen-oktent
tomorrow afternoon	**morgenmiddag** mor-hen-mid-duk
tomorrow evening	**morgenavond** mor-hen-ahvent
the day after tomorrow	**overmorgen** over-mor-hen

MONTHS AND DATES

January	**Januari**
	yun-oo-*ah*-ree
February	**februari**
	fay-broo-*ah*-ree
March	**maart**
	mart
April	**april**
	ah-pril
May	**mei**
	may
June	**juni**
	yoo-nee
July	**juli**
	yoo-lee
August	**augustus**
	ow-h*e*rs-tes
September	**september**
	september
October	**oktober**
	oktober
November	**november**
	november
December	**december**
	day-s*e*mber
in January	**in januari**
	in yun-oo-*ah*-ree
until February	**tot februari**
	tot fay-broo-*ah*-ree
before March	**vóór maart**
	vor mart
after April	**na april**
	na ah-pril
during May	**gedurende mei**
	her-d*oo*-render may
not until June	**niet tot juni**
	neet tot *yoo*-nee
the beginning of July	**begin juli**
	ber-hin *yoo*-lee
middle of August	**midden augustus**
	midden ow-h*e*rs-tes

end of September	**eind September**
	*e*ynt september
last month	**verleden maand**
	ver-l*a*den mahnt
this month	**deze maand**
	d*a*zer mahnt
next month	**volgende maand**
	vol-hender mahnt
in spring	**in de lente**
	in der l*e*nter
in summer	**in de zomer**
	in der z*o*mer
in autumn	**in de herfst**
	in der hairfst
in winter	**in de winter**
	in der w*i*nter
this year	**dit jaar**
	dit yar
last year	**verleden jaar**
	ver-l*a*den yar
next year	**volgend jaar**
	vol-hent yar
in 1982	**in negentien (honderd) tweën-tachtig**
	in n*a*yhenteen (hondert) tway-en-t*u*ktik
in 1985	**in negentien (honderd) vijfen-tachtig**
	in n*a*yhenteen (hondert) v*e*yf-en-t*u*ktik
in 1990	**in negentien (honderd) negentig**
	in n*a*yhenteen (hondert) n*a*yhentik
What is the date today?	**Wat is de datum vandaag?**
	wut is der d*a*h-tum vun-dahk
It's the 6th of March	**Het is zes maart**
	et is zes mart
It's the 12th of April	**Het is twaalf april**
	et is twahlf ah-pr*i*l
It's the 21st of August	**Het is éénentwintig augustus**
	et is *a*yn-en-tintik ow-h*e*rs-tes

Public holidays

● Shops, schools and offices are closed on the following dates:

1 January	**Nieuwjaarsdag**	New Year's Day
...	**Paasmaandag**	Easter Monday
	Pinkstermaandag	Whitsun Monday
	Hemelvaartsdag	Ascension Day
30 April	**Koninginnedag**	The Queen's birthday
25 December	**Eerste Kerstdag**	Christmas Day
26 December	**Tweede Kerstdag**	Boxing Day
5 May	**Bevrijdingsdag**	Liberation Day
		(once every 5 years)

COUNTRIES AND NATIONALITIES
Countries

America	**Amerika** ah-m*a*y-ree-ka
Australia	**Australië** ah-oo-str*ah*-lee-yer
Austria	**Oostenrijk** *o*h-sten-reyk
Belgium	**België** b*e*l-hee-yer
Britain	**Groot Brittannië** hrote brit-t*u*n-yer
Canada	**Canada** c*a*hnada
Czechoslovakia	**Tsjecho-Slowakije** cheko-slovuk-eeyer
East Africa	**Oost Afrika** ohst *ah*-free-kah
East Germany	**Oost Duitsland** ohst d*o*-eets-lunt
Eire	**Ierland** *ee*r-lunt
England	**Engeland** *e*ng-er-lunt
France	**Frankrijk** fr*u*nk-reyk
Greece	**Griekenland** hr*ee*-ken-lunt
India .	**India** *i*ndee-yah
Indonesia	**Indonesië** indo-n*a*y-see-yer
Italy	**Italië** ee-t*ah*-lee-yer
Luxembourg	**Luxemburg** l*oo*ksem-burk
The Netherlands	**Nederland** n*a*y-der-lunt
New Zealand	**Nieuw Zeeland** neew z*a*y-lunt
Pakistan	**Pakistan** pah-kee-st*u*n

Poland	**Polen**
	poh-len
Portugal	**Portugal**
	por-too-hul
Scotland	**Schotland**
	skot-lunt
South Africa	**Zuid Afrika**
	zo-eet ah-free-kah
Spain	**Spanje**
	spun-yer
Surinam	**Suriname**
	soo-ree-nah-mer
Switzerland	**Zwitserland**
	zwitser-lunt
Wales	**Wales**
	wayls
West Germany	**West Duitsland**
	west do-eets-lunt
West Indies	**West Indië**
	west indee-yer
Yugoslavia	**Joego-Slavië**
	yoo-hoh-slah-vee-yer

Nationalities
[*Use the first alternative for men, the second for women*]

American	**amerikaan/amerikaanse**
	ah-may-ree-k*a*hn/ah-may-ree-k*a*hn-ser
Australian	**australiër/australische**
	ah-oo-str*a*h-lee-yer/ah-oo-str*a*h-lee-ser
British	**brit/britse**
	brit/br*i*tser
Canadian	**canadees/canadese**
	cahna-d*a*ys/cahna-d*a*yser
East African	**oost afrikaner/oost afrikaanse**
	ohst-ah-free-k*a*hner/ohst ah-free-k*a*hn-ser
English	**engelsman/engelse**
	*e*ng-els-mun/*e*ng-el-ser
Indian	**indiër/indische**
	*i*ndee-yer/*i*ndee-ser
Irish	**ier/ierse**
	eer/*ee*r-ser
New Zealander	**nieuw zeelander/nieuw zeelandse**
	neew-z*a*y-lunter/neew-z*a*y-lunt-ser
Pakistani	**pakistaner/pakistaanse**
	puk-kee-stah-ner/puk-kee-st*a*hn-ser
Scots	**schot/schotse**
	skot/sk*o*tser
South African	**zuid afrikaner/zuid afrikanse**
	z*o*-eet ah-free-k*a*hner/z*o*-eet ah-free-k*a*hn-ser
Welsh	**welliser**
	w*e*llee-ser
West Indian	**west indiër/west indische**
	west *i*ndee-yer/west *i*ndee-ser

DEPARTMENT STORE GUIDE

Aardewerk	Earthenware
Baby uitzet	Layette
Bedden	Beds
Beneden verdieping	Ground floor
Blouses	Blouses
Boeken	Books
Camping	Camping
Cadeaux	Gifts
Ceintuurs	Belts
Corsetten	Girdles
Dames modes	Ladies' fashions
Dassen	Ties
Dekens	Blankets
Derde verdieping	Third floor
Diepvries	Frozen food
Doe-het-zelf afdeling	DIY department
Eerste verdieping	First floor
Electriciteits-benodigdheden	Electrical appliances
Etenswaren	Food
Fietsen	Bicycles
Fotografie	Photography
Fournituren	Haberdashery
Fruit	Fruit
Geschenken	Gifts
Glaswerk	Glassware
Gordijnen	Curtains
Grammofoonplaten	Records
Handschoenen	Gloves
Handwerken	Needlework
Heren confectie/modes	Men's fashions
Ijzerwaren	Hardware
Inlichtingen	Information/inquiries
Juwelen	Jewellery
Keuken inrichting	Kitchen furniture
Kinderkleding	Children's clothes
Knippatronen	Paper patterns
Kousen	Hosiery
Kussens	Cushions/pillows
Lederwaren	Leather goods
Linnen	Linen
Lingerie	Lingerie

Meubels	Furniture
Overhemden	Shirts
Panties	Tights
Parfumerieën	Perfumery
Parterre	Ground floor
Porcelein	China
Pullovers	Pullovers
Radio	Radio
Reisartikelen	Travel goods
Riemen	Belts
Schrijfbenodigdheden	Stationery
Schoenen	Shoes
Schoonheidsmiddelen	Cosmetics
Schoonmaakartikelen	Cleaning materials
Souterrain	Basement
Speelgoed	Toys
Sportartikelen	Sports goods
Stofferingen	Draperies
Tabaksartikelen	Tobacco
Tapijten	Carpets
Televisie	Television
Tweede verdieping	Second floor
Vierde verdieping	Fourth floor
Wol	Woollens

CONVERSION TABLES

Read the centre column of these tables from right to left to convert from metric to imperial and from left to right to convert from imperial to metric e.g. 5 litres = 8.80 pints; 5 pints = 2.84 litres.

pints		litres		gallons		litres
1.76	1	0.57		0.22	1	4.55
3.52	2	1.14		0.44	2	9.09
5.28	3	1.70		0.66	3	13.64
7.07	4	2.27		0.88	4	18.18
8.80	5	2.84		1.00	5	22.73
10.56	6	3.41		1.32	6	27.28
12.32	7	3.98		1.54	7	31.82
14.08	8	4.55		1.76	8	36.37
15.84	9	5.11		1.98	9	40.91

ounces		grams		pounds		kilos
0.04	1	28.35		2.20	1	0.45
0.07	2	56.70		4.41	2	0.91
0.11	3	85.05		6.61	3	1.36
0.14	4	113.40		8.82	4	1.81
0.18	5	141.75		11.02	5	2.27
0.21	6	170.10		13.23	6	2.72
0.25	7	198.45		15.43	7	3.18
0.28	8	226.80		17.64	8	3.63
0.32	9	225.15		19.84	9	4.08

inches		centimetres		yards		metres
0.39	1	2.54		1.09	1	0.91
0.79	2	5.08		2.19	2	1.83
1.18	3	7.62		3.28	3	2.74
1.58	4	10.16		4.37	4	3.66
1.97	5	12.70		5.47	5	4.57
2.36	6	15.24		6.56	6	5.49
2.76	7	17.78		7.66	7	6.40
3.15	8	20.32		8.65	8	7.32
3.54	9	22.86		9.84	9	8.23

miles		kilometres
0.62	1	1.61
1.24	2	3.22
1.86	3	4.83
2.49	4	6.44
3.11	5	8.05
3.73	6	9.66
4.35	7	11.27
4.97	8	12.87
5.59	9	14.48

A quick way to convert kilometres to miles: divide by 8 and multiply by 5. To convert miles to kilometres: divide by 5 and multiply by 8.

fahrenheit (°F)	centigrade (°C)	lbs/ sq in	k/ sq cm
212°	100° boiling point	18	1.3
100°	38°	20	1.4
94.8°	36.9° body temperature	22	1.5
86°	30°	25	1.7
77°	25°	29	2.0
68°	20°	32	2.3
59°	15°	35	2.5
50°	10°	36	2.5
41°	5°	39	2.7
32°	0° freezing point	40	2.8
14°	−10°	43	3.0
−4°	−20°	45	3.2
		46	3.2
		50	3.5
		60	4.2

To convert °C to °F: divide by 5, multiply by 9 and add 32. To convert °F to °C: take away 32, divide by 9 and multiply by 5.

CLOTHING SIZES

Remember – always try on clothes before buying. Clothing sizes are usually unreliable.

women's dresses and suits

Europe	38	40	42	44	46	48
UK	32	34	36	38	40	42
USA	10	12	14	16	18	20

men's suits and coats

Europe	46	48	50	52	54	56
UK and USA	36	38	40	42	44	46

men's shirts

Europe	36	37	38	39	41	42	43
UK and USA	14	14½	15	15½	16	16½	17

socks

Europe	38–39	39–40	40–41	41–42	42–43
UK and USA	9½	10	10½	11	11½

shoes

Europe	34	35½	36½	38	39	41	42	43	44	45
UK	2	3	4	5	6	7	8	9	10	11
USA	3½	4½	5½	6½	7½	8½	9½	10½	11½	12½

Do it yourself

Some notes on the language

This section does not deal with 'grammar' as such. The purpose here is to explain some of the most obvious and elementary nuts and bolts of the language, based on the principal phrases included in the book. This information should enable you to produce numerous sentences of your own making, although you will obviously still be fairly limited in what you can say.

There is no pronunciation guide in this section, partly because it would get in the way of the explanations and partly because you have to do it yourself at this stage if you are serious – work out the pronunciation from all the earlier examples.

THE

All nouns in Dutch belong to one of two genders: common (originally masculine or feminine) or neuter, irrespective of whether they refer to living beings or inanimate objects.

the	common	neuter	plural
the address		het adres	de adressen/the addresses
the apple	de appel		de appels/the apples
the bill	de rekening		de rekeningen/the bills
the cup of tea	de kop thee		de koppen thee/the cups of tea
the glass of beer		het glas bier	de glazen bier/the glasses of beer
the key	de sleutel		de sleutels/the keys
the luggage	de bagage		
the menu		het menu	de menu's/the menus
the newspaper	de krant		de kranten/the newspapers
the sandwich	de dubbele boterham		de dubbele boterhammen/ the sandwiches
the suitcase	de koffer		de koffers/the suitcases
the telephone directory		het telefoon boek	de telefoon boeken/the telephone directories
the timetable	de dienstregeling		de dienstregelingen/the timetables

Important things to remember

- *The* is **de** before a common noun, and **het** before a neuter singular noun.
- There is no way of telling if a noun is common or neuter. You have to learn and remember its gender. Obviously if you are reading a word with **de** or **het** in front of it you can tell its gender immediately: **de appel** is common (*c.* in dictionaries) and **het menu** is neuter (*n.* in dictionaries).
- Does it matter? Not unless you want to make a serious attempt to speak correctly and scratch beneath the surface of the language. You would be understood if you said **de menu** or even **het appel**, providing your pronunciation was good.
- There is one exception however: all diminutives are neuter; they end in **-je** or **-tje**.
- *The* is always **de** before a noun in the plural.
- As a general rule, a noun adds an 's' or 'en' to become plural. But watch out for the many exceptions such as **kind/kinderen**, **menu/menu's**.
- In Dutch, as in English, luggage has no plural.

Practise saying and writing these sentences in Dutch:

Have you got the key?	**Heeft u de sleutel?**
Have you got the luggage?	**Heeft u . . .?**
Have you got the telephone directory?	
Have you got the menu?	
I'd like the key	**Ik zou graag de sleutel**
I'd like the luggage	**Ik zou graag . . .**
I'd like the bill	
I'd like the keys	
Where is the key?	**Waar is de sleutel?**
Where is the timetable?	**Waar is . . .?**
Where is the address?	
Where is the suitcase?	
Where are the keys?	**Waar zijn de sleutels?**
Where are the sandwiches?	**Waar zijn . . .?**
Where are the apples?	
Where are the suitcases?	
Where is the luggage?	**Waar is . . .?**
Where can I get the key?	**Waar kan ik de sleutel krijgen?**
Where can I get the address?	**Waar kan ik . . . krijgen?**
Where can I get the timetables?	

Now make up more sentences along the same lines. Try adding *please*: **alstublieft**, at the end.

A/AN

a/an	singular	plural	some/any
an address	een adres	addressen	addresses
an apple	een appel	appels	apples
a bill	een rekening	rekeningen	bills
a cup of tea	een kop thee	koppen thee	cups of tea
a glass of beer	een glas bier	glazen bier	glasses of beer
a key	een sleutel	sleutels	keys
...	de bagage	...	luggage
a menu	een menu	menu's	menus
a newspaper	een krant	kranten	newspapers
a sandwich	een dubbele boterham	dubbele botterhammen	sandwiches
a suitcase	een koffer	koffers	suitcases
a telephone directory	een telefoon boek	telefoon boeken	telephone directories
a timetable	een dienstregeling	dienstregelingen	timetables

Important things to remember

- *A* or *an* is always **een** before a noun, whether common or neuter.
- *Some* or *any* before a noun in the plural has no equivalent in Dutch. Just leave it out. Examples of this can be seen in the phrases marked* below.

Practise saying and writing these sentences in Dutch:

Have you got a bill?	**Heeft u . . .?**
Have you got a menu?	
I'd like a telephone directory	**Ik zou graag . . .**
*I'd like some sandwiches	
*Where can I get some newspapers?	**Waar kan ik . . . krijgen?**
Where can I get a cup of tea?	
Is there a key?	**Is er een sleutel?**
Is there a timetable?	**Is er . . .?**
Is there a telephone directory?	
Is there a menu?	

*Are there any keys?	**Zijn er sleutels?**
*Are there any newspapers?	**Zijn er . . .?**
*Are there any sandwiches?	

Now make up more sentences along the same lines. Then try these new phrases:

Ik wil graag . . . (I'll have . . .)
Ik heb . . . nodig (I need . . .)

I'll have a glass of beer	**Ik wil graag een glas bier**
I'll have a cup of tea	**Ik will graag . . .**
I'll have some apples	
I need a cup of tea	**Ik heb een kop thee nodig**
I need a key	**Ik heb . . . nodig**
*I need some newspapers	**Ik heb kranten nodig**
*I need some keys	
*I need some addresses	
*I need some sandwiches	
*I need some suitcases	

SOME/ANY

In cases where *some* or *any* refer to more than one thing, such as *some/any newspapers* and *some/any tomatoes*, there is no Dutch equivalent, as explained earlier.

(some/any) newspapers	**kranten**
(some/any) tomatoes	**tomaten**

As a guide, you can usually *count* the number of containers or whole items. In cases where *some* refers to a part of a whole thing or an indefinite quantity, the word **wat** can be used.

Look at the list below and complete the missing items

the butter	de boter	wat boter	some butter
the bread	het brood	wat brood	some bread
the cheese	de kaas	wat kaas	some cheese
the coffee	de koffie	wat koffie	some coffee
the ice-cream	het ijs	...	some ice-cream
the lemonade	de limonade	...	some lemonade
the pineapple	de ananas	...	some pineapple
the sugar	de suiker	...	some sugar
the tea	de thee	...	some tea
the water	het water	...	some water
the wine	de wijn	...	some wine

Practise saying and writing these sentences in Dutch:

Have you got some ice-cream	Heeft u wat ijs?
Have you got some pineapple?	
I'd like some butter	Ik zou wat boter
I'd like some sugar	
I'd like some bread	
Where can I get some cheese?	Waar kan ik wat kaas krijgen?
Where can I get some ice-cream?	
Where can I get some water?	
Is there any water?	Is er wat water?
Is there any lemonade?	
Is there any wine?	
I'll have some beer	Ik wil graag wat bier
I'll have some tea	
I'll have some coffee	

THIS AND THAT

There are two words you can use when pointing:
dit (this), dat (that)
If you don't know the Dutch name for an object, just point and say:

Ik zou graag dat	I'd like that
Ik wil graag dit	I'll have this
Ik heb dat nodig	I need that

HELPING OTHERS

You can help yourself with phrases such as:

I'd like . . . a sandwich	**Ik zou graag . . . een dubbele boterham**
Where can I get . . . a cup of tea?	**Waar kan ik . . . een kop thee . . . krijgen?**
I'll have . . . a glass of beer	**Ik will graag . . . een glas bier**
I need . . . a bill	**Ik heb . . . een rekening . . . nodig**

If you find a compatriot having trouble making himself/herself understood, you should be able to speak to the Dutch person on his/her behalf. A pronunciation guide is provided from here on.

He'd like . . .	**Hij zou graag een cake**
	hey zow hrahk en cake
She'd like . . .	**Zij zou graag een cake**
	zey zow hrahk en cake
Where can he get . . .?	**Waar kan hij een kop thee krijgen?**
	war kun hey en kop tay krey-hen
Where can she get . . .?	**Waar kan zij een kop thee krijgen?**
	war kun zey en kop tay krey-hen
He'll have . . .	**Hij wil graag een glas bier**
	hey wil hrahk en hlus beer
She'll have . . .	**Zij wil graag een glas bier**
	zey wil hrahk en hlus beer
He needs . . .	**Hij heeft zeep nodig**
	hey hayft zape nodik
She needs . . .	**Zij heeft zeep nodig**
	zey hayft zape nodik

You can also help a couple or a group if they are having difficulties. The Dutch word for *they* is **zij**.

They'd like . . .	**Zij willen graag een krant**
	zey willen hrahk en krunt
Where can they get . . .?	**Waar kunnen zij een reisgids krijgen?**
	wahr koonen zey en reys-hits krey-hen
They'll have . . .	**Zij willen graag wat brood**
	zey willen hrahk wut brote
They need . . .	**Zij hebben wat wijn nodig**
	zey hebben wut weyn nodik

What about the two of you? No problem. The word for *we* is **wij**.

We'd like . . .	**Wij willen graag wat wijn** wey willen hrahk wut weyn
Where can we get . . .?	**Waar kunnen wij sleutels krijgen?** wahr koonen wey slertels krey-hen
We'll have . . .	**Wij willen graag het menu** wey willen hrahk et mer-noo
We need . . .	**Wij hebben de rekening nodig** wey hebben der rayker-ning nodik

Try writing out your own checklist for these four useful phrase-starters like this:

Ik zou graag . . .   **Wij willen graag . . .**
Hij zou graag . . .   **Zij willen graag . . .**
Zij zou graag . . .
Waar kan ik . . . krijgen?   **Waar kunnen wij . . . krijgen?**
Waar kan hij . . . krijgen?   **Waar kunnen zij . . . krijgen?**
Waar kan zij . . . krijgen?

MORE PRACTICE

Here are some useful Dutch names of things. See how many different sentences you can make up, using the various points of information given earlier in this section.

		singular	plural
1	ashtray	**asbak** (*c*)	**asbakken**
2	bag	**tas** (*c*)	**tassen**
3	car	**auto** (*c*)	**auto's**
4	cigarette	**sigaret** (*c*)	**sigaretten**
5	corkscrew	**kurketrekker** (*c*)	**kurketrekkers**
6	deckchair	**ligstoel** (*c*)	**ligstoelen**
7	garage (repairs)	**garage** (*c*)	**garages**
8	grapes	**druif** (*c*)	**druiven**
9	ice-cream	**ijsje** (*n*)	**ijsjes**
10	melon	**meloen** (*c*)	**meloenen**
11	passport	**paspoort** (*n*)	**paspoorten**
12	drying-up cloth	**theedoek** (*c*)	**theedoeken**
13	salad (lettuce)	**krop sla** (*c*)	**kroppen sla**
14	shoe	**schoen** (*c*)	**schoenen**
15	stamp	**postzegel** (*c*)	**postzegels**
16	station	**station** (*n*)	**stations**
17	sunglasses	**zonnebril** (*c*)	**zonnebrillen**
18	telephone	**telefoon** (*c*)	**telefoons**
19	ticket	**kaartje** (*n*)	**kaartjes**

Index

Arthur Eperon
Travellers' Italy

A whole variety of holiday routes to guarantee that you eat, drink, explore
and relax in the places the Italians themselves would choose: the best
places to sample local speciality foods and wines, spectacular scenery,
facts the history books won't tell you, as well as the magnificent beaches
and art treasures you'd expect. Arthur Eperon is one of the best-known
travel writers in Europe and has an extensive knowledge of Italy and its
food and wine. With an introduction by Frank Bough.

Arthur Eperon
Travellers' France

Six major routes across France, taking in the best restaurants and hotels,
visiting the most interesting out-of-the-way places. This detailed and up-to-
the-minute handbook is for the traveller who wants more out of France
than a mad dash down the motorway. Each of the six routes across the
country is illustrated with a specially-commissioned two-colour map, and
includes a host of information on where to eat and drink, where to take
children, where to stay, and how to get the most out of the towns and
countryside. .

Ken Welsh
Hitch-Hiker's Guide to Europe

The new and completely updated edition of this invaluable guide covers
Europe, North Africa and the Middle East. Ken Welsh gives advice on
routes to take, what to take, eating, sleeping, local transport, what to see,
together with information on currency, useful phrases and working abroad.

'Hitch-hikers will adopt it as their travelling bible but it's amusing and
informative for those who fancy more traditional ways'   BBC

edited by Harriet Peacock
The Alternative Holiday Catalogue

If you're looking for a holiday that you won't find in a travel agent's window. . .if there's something you've always wanted to try your hand at. . .or if you want to take your special interest on holiday with you, this A-to-Z of ideas and information is the book you need. 150 different types of special-interest holiday, from backgammon and Bible-study to Zen, upholstery and giving up smoking. This book tells you where to go, what to take, what it costs, and what you'll find when you get there.

John Slater
Just Off for the Weekend
Slater's hotel guide

The bestselling author of *Just Off the Motorway* has selected more than a hundred places to stay, with details of what to see and walks to take, specially recommended pubs and restaurants – and all within a Friday evening's drive from one of England's big cities. With an introduction by Anna Ford.

John Slater
Just Off the Motorway

The new and enlarged edition of a sensational bestseller.
Introduction by Russell Harty.

Here's the new, bang-up-to-date edition of the handbook everyone needs. Detailed research, careful sampling, and more than 150 maps show where you can find any service you require – cheaper and better – by turning off at a junction and driving no more than three miles off the motorway – eating, drinking, overnight stops, breakdown services, petrol, visits.

'Worth a detour to buy it' DAILY MAIL

Harrap's New Pocket French and English Dictionary

The classic French/English and English/French reference for students and travellers, this edition contains some 4,500 entries in each language, including all the principal words in current use – recent additions to both languages, scientific terms, tourist expressions. Entries also contain phonetic renderings and examples of idiomatic usage.

A Multilingual Commercial Dictionary

Some 3,000 words and phrases in common commercial use are listed in English, French, German, Spanish and Portuguese followed by their translation in the other languages. The equivalent American expression is also included where relevant. Simple to use and invaluable for everyday reference, the dictionary covers terms used throughout banking, accounting, insurance, shipping, export and import and international trade.